What the Raags told me

What the Raags told me

Vasudev Murthy

Rupa & Co

Text Copyright © *Vasudev Murthy* 2004

Illustrations Copyright © *Inner Voice*

Published in 2004 by

Rupa & Co

7/16 Ansari Road, Daryaganj
New Delhi 110 002

Sales Centres:
Allahabad • Bangalore • Chandigarh
• Chennai • Hyderabad
• Jaipur • Kathmandu • Kolkata
• Mumbai • Pune

Printed in India by: Gopsons Papers
Limited, NOIDA

Designed for the publisher by
INNER VOICE, MUMBAI

Creative direction
ASHOK ROY

Illustrations
BAPU PAIL

Page design
KISHORE ESHWAR

Technical support
T. S. RASHEED

To
Vidya
A Living Raag

Shadaj
Rishabh
Gandhar
Madhyam
Pancham
Dhaivat
Nishad

Music is
the sound
of God.

Contents

Foreword

Dear Readers,

Indian Raags have a great history behind them. They are the combinations of different swaras (notes) arranged in a systematic pattern. If rendered to perfection, they can create wonders. Thus Raag Malhar can invite rain in any season and Raag Deepak can light lamps if sung with the right intensity and purity of purpose. They can create different moods and emotions as well as a sense of time.

When my able student Vasudev came to me with the thought that the Raags, which I have taught him, had said something to him, I was taken aback. It aroused my curiosity. Over and above, he wanted all the conversations to be put in words and write a book on his unique experiences. A book on how to play Indian music on the violin, a book on the technical differences between playing the violin in the Indian and Western styles - these titles of a book one can easily understand, but a book with the title "What the Raags told me" - the whole idea was unique and novel. He wanted my permission to go ahead with the project. To be frank, though I did give my permission, it was with a certain degree of doubt in my mind.

Let me tell the readers that when the complete work came before me and I went through it with the help of my students and family (due to my ill health), I felt proud to be the Guru of such a brilliant student. When you go through the book page by page, you come to know his honesty, sincerity and imagination. The whole book is a piece of art, which shows his emotions, character, and his love for music, Indian culture and his personal devotion. His poetic description and imagination has shown the characteristics of each Raag described in this book with their right moods and behaviour.

It would have been "Sone pe suhaga" if Vasudev had taken music as his main career. But looking at the way he has written this book, I have no doubts that in his chosen career, he must be creating harmonics and wonders. I also wish that he would consider many more Raags for a future project. I wish him success and hope he will be a good and popular violinist. My blessings are with him.

God bless you.

Pandit V. G. Jog

September 2003

(Pandit V.G.Jog passed away on the 31st of January 2004 in Kolkata)

A Note by the Author

The idea for this work was triggered during a train journey between Chennai and Bangalore in early 2002. I was going through one of the late Kumar Gandharva's books and was lost in admiration for his lovely compositions. For a day or two after I returned, I kept turning towards the tunes and felt profoundly moved by theiir beauty and lyrical messages. I feld impelled to convert the messages into words. The first two or three chapters flowed in a rush. Then there was hiatus of few months while I waited for feedback from my friends at the Jacaranda Press. On receiving encouragement to continue from them and my Guru, Pandit V.G.Jog, I completed the rest in a space of a few weeks.

To be sure, the idea had been germinating in my mind for a very long time. The late Kumar Gandharva, the late Nikhil Bannerjee and Pandit V.G.Jog's music had always taken me to a zone of pure pleasure, through a spectrum of agonizing emotions. Many private recordings of my own Guru's concerts remain today as the epitome of musical creativity and absolute genius—I recall in particular a recording of Raag Bageshree and another of Jhinjhoti. The exploration of Raags always seemed to involve a kind of storytelling, beautifully agonizing in the sense of not knowing what they were saying but still being profoundly disturbed by them.

Of my Guru, Pandit Jog, I can never have enough to say. Though I met him relatively late in his life, he gave me whatever he could without hesitation. His fame as a violinist needs no reference, but his extraordinary abilities as a teacher par-excellence are probably not as well known. A few simple words, a few points in helping compare Raags—and an ocean opened up. He has been everything one might have idealized in a Guru. His deep knowledge and a willingness to give all, his personal simplicity and decency and a love for this students, all who came into contact with him can never forget these traits. Whatever you find correct in this book is entirely to his credit, whatever you find incorrect, a reflection of my own personal inadequecies as a student.

I thank Pandit Jog's wonderful family for encouraging this project. And I thank my other - more gifted and talented - fellow students who have enriched my musical explorations unselfishly.

I thank my mother for instilling in me a love for music, which has always been its own reward.

I thank my wife Vidya for her encouragement and for creating an atmosphere, which permitted this project to progress. This book would have remained in my head had she not pushed me to write it.

I thank my little son, Sarang, for just being himself!

Finally, my thanks to the fine folk at Jacaranda Press and Rupa and Co. who have made this work possible.

Vasudev Murthy

Conventions used

It is not necessary to have a theoretical knowledge of music in order to be able to read this book, but for those interested in deciphering the notations, certain conventions are explained.

The musical notes in this book are expressed in the following manner.

Shadaj	S	
Rishabh	komal: r	Shuddha: R
Gandhar	komal: g	Shuddha: G
Madhyam	Shuddha: M	teevra: m
Pancham	P	
Dhaivat	komal: d	Shuddha: D
Nishad	komal: n	Shuddha: N

Notes in the higher octave (Taar Saptak) have a "⌃" next to them on the right. For example: g⌃, would mean komal Gandhar in the Taar Saptak.

Notes in the lower octave (Mandra Saptak) have a "." next to them on the left below them. For example: .N, would mean Shuddha Nishad in the Mandra Saptak.

A hyphen indicates that the note is extended; it has carried over from the previous beat.

h! My wonderful fortune! To be born in this land with such music that could only have been showered from the heavens!

Every morning, before dawn, I sat meditating. After years of becoming possessed by the magic of silence, I added my Tanpura. It did not distract me at all. Soon my fingers moved mechanically - almost independently - strumming the strings

P S S ˬ S

Did they understand my mission? I think so. My meditation sessions became even more enjoyable and intense. The energy within me flowed like never before. Each plucked string vibrated with a life all its own and the sound started to soften and vanish, but not before another plucked string announced its presence, with respect for the others and dignity of its own.

The sounds played on the cells in my body and the harmony was indescribable. Each seemed to reach out and snatch the results of the Tanpura's benevolence. After many, many such sessions, when I was past middle-age, I felt something grow within myself. I observed it neutrally and saw its struggle to identify itself and break free. I knew what it was and why it had come.

Soon, I let my spirit come out. It sat gently like a petal in my palm and asked me what I wanted it to do. And I asked it to go and wander through this blessed land and learn about its music and tell me about it. Where did these Raags come from? Why had they come and what did they have to say?

And so my spirit soared to the blue sky and went on its journey. One moment it was in the East and then the West. Then the South and then the North. There was no method. It simply closed its eyes and swirled and dived as it pleased, listening, listening. Listening to the sounds and songs of India. And pointing at the spirit of the Raags that had lent themselves to that divine music.

It skimmed the rivers, first hugging the shores and then crossing them, early in the morning. It went along the deserts and basked in that unbearable heat which paralysed even the air. It went to the villages and the fields and understood the green tones. It entered the fishing nets of the villages by the seashores and nodded as it heard the sounds of the sea and of the men who sang to the fishes. It sat in temple bells and heard them ring and send out their pure notes to the rest of the Universe. And it listened to the songs that people sang in those temples and Gurdwaras and touched the tears that formed and made their way down to the earth that welcomed them. It heard the rhythms and lilts of men who went with *Ektaras* from village to village deep inside India, lost in their own ecstasy seeking nothing as gross as money or fame. It listened to mothers singing to babies in their laps, holding their hands and gently releasing them into the comfort and protection of sleep. It listened to beggars on the streets asking God, during sleepless nights, why He had punished them in this way and why He did not take pity on them. It listened to pious men singing alone in their windowless rooms asking to be delivered from the wearing cycle of day and night. It sat respectfully by the cremation ground picking up the deep sadness of the mourners and the dignity of the religious chants.

and let the drops fall on my face, washing away both dust and despair.

My spirit and I danced in the rain

RR $_{n}$ $_{n}$ S, nPMR $_{n}$ S

aag Megh conclusively threw out any despondent, nostalgic and melancholic moods I still wished to keep with me, the pretentious philosopher. The celebration of rain, the joy of nature and of all living beings rescued from heat - no Raag could keep my mood dim and sulking any longer!

My spirit too had shaken away the cloaks of doom and gloom and proclaimed the victory of joy! Between creation and destruction, surely there was the beauty of existence - here and now! When I meditated, even my equanimity had the colour of a smile! No wonder I felt energized and refreshed all day long and thought that God had reserved his blessings for those who knew how to laugh.

Two summers ago, when I had turned eighty, I went to the nearby forest for long strolls, alone with my spirit. It danced around the trunks of trees and leapt up into the branches. It wrapped itself in green leaves and inquired in the hives of bees. Baby birds had grown and had ambitions of conquering the skies. Their parents tried to teach them patience, but invariably, one or the other youngster came tumbling down the side of a tall tree! I watched all this with a smile. Perspiration poured down my face, but I walked on, taking in the fragrance of the forest. Who knew how many more such summers I would be able to enjoy? The time to experience everything was now!

As I sat at the top of a hillock at the foot of a tall tree, catching my breath and looking down upon the little village far below in the valley, I wondered about the paradox. Heat was unwelcome in one place and loved in another. I had happily subjected myself to an arduous walk in mid-summer in the afternoon and I saw every merit in it!

My spirit too ran away. As I wiped my face with a handkerchief, I saw that it had returned with not one but two guests! It was strange, but they seemed to be echoes of the sounds within my heart!

A peacock and a young male deer stood right in front of me. My spirit straddled both, insolently. The peacock moved restlessly on its feet and the deer shook his antlers from side to side. And I saw that they were not what they seemed to be.

"We are the Sarangs!" a collective voice rang out.

"We cannot stop for even a moment! We must move on and on! Is it not wrong to waste the energy given to us by God by simply resting and sleeping?"

The peacock spoke alone: *"It is the time to explore what life is all about! I am curious! I live and must experience it fully! I have no time for idle philosophising!*

See my beautiful feathers as I spread my fan and shake them! I am happy, oh so happy, to be alive and experience small joys! Only yesterday, it rained ever so briefly and I was thrilled!

I must rush from tree to tree, bush to bush! I must exaggerate the dangers I face! Look at me! Admire me!

My energy and vibrancy is in Shadaj, Shuddha Rishabh, Shuddha Madhyam and Pancham. I proclaim the news of the zenith of my existence with Shuddha Nishad, Shadaj, Shuddha Rishabh, Shadaj, Komal Nishad and Pancham again! Who has the time to dwell morbidly in the lower octaves?

Who has the time to linger on each note when the next note beckons so urgently? Who has the time to rest at the stately Shuddha Gandhar? Not me!

I gave my feathers to Krishna when he came to this forest! And he wears them wherever he is and whatever he does - does this not prove my loveliness? I, Brindavani Sarang, am the joyous gift of the heavens!"

The deer looked askance at the pirouetting capricious peacock. *"Look at my antlers, silly bird! Which craftsman but Vishwakarma himself could make such designs? I reign over the veldt and let smaller birds rest on me! I do not destroy, I do not create chaos like you! But all know my strength and vigour! Who in this forest, nay this Universe, can run as swiftly and beautifully as me, Shuddha Sarang?*

In the languid afternoons, Teevra Madhyam, Pancham, Shuddha Madhyam and a long and caressing Shuddha Rishabh suggest rest. The heat is welcome; it gives all an excuse to retreat to the shades of trees and recoup their strength after the happy explorations of the morning! And I express these simple pleasures with Shadaj, Shuddha Nishad, Shuddha Dhaivat, Pancham, Teevra Madhyam and Shuddha Rishabh!

Where you run about in circles preening, enchanted by your own beauty, foolish Peacock, I rub my flank on the bark of the trees and give them pleasure too! I sat next to Sita when she lived in this forest with her twins, Lav and Kush and she herself stroked my broad, lovely forehead!"

"Are you done, O absurd Deer? In my silken feathers, which I spread out for others to admire and truly understand the beauties of life, you will find all my notes sprinkled randomly! Up here, near my crown, I have placed Shuddha Rishabh, Shuddha Madhyam, Pancham, Shuddha Madhyam, Shuddha Rishabh and Pancham, swirling and dazzling! On my velvet crop are the higher notes, Shuddha Rishabh, Shuddha Madhyam, Shuddha Rishabh, Shadaj, Shuddha Rishabh and Shadaj, with shades of violet, green and blue! My eyes are the lustrous Shuddha and Komal Nishads, untouched by any trace of pathos! Pancham, bright and beautiful is at the centre of each feather!

I have sat at the feet of the Gods and allowed them to sing me when their joy bubbles over! Sing me in the middle and upper octaves, never resting! I am quick and restless, ever happy!"

"Perhaps," said the deer. *"But my eyes are the two Madhyams, liquid and lovely. Pancham sits boldly on my powerful antlers, held to my handsome head by Shuddha Rishabh. I speed effortlessly through the forests, sure-footed. My thick glossy coat is made of Teevra Madhyam, Pancham, Shuddha Dhaivat, Shuddha Madhyam and Shuddha Rishabh! And my fawn is always protected and reassured by Shuddha Madhyam, Shuddha Rishabh, Shuddha Nishad, Shadaj and Shuddha Nishad. Where you, Brindavani Sarang, are always thinking only of yourself, I assert my handsome vitality by protecting others!*

"O Deer! Why should we mock at each other? The Summer is here and life is to be enjoyed! For both of us, Shuddha Rishabh and Pancham are the tones of bright energy. Let us play with each other! Each is more beautiful than the next!"

I watched agape and with delight this dialogue between the two most charismatic inhabitants of the forest! Two brilliant Raags had come together and showered me with bliss. Teasing one moment, pleading the next, but ever frenetic and refusing to rest, they taught me an important lesson.

The afternoon ghosts moved away, not having any more time to spend in sharing their secrets with others. I saw my spirit jump on the antlers of the deer and then quickly rustle through the long and sweeping feathers of the peacock before returning to me in a rush.

As they left, I heard them sing a quick and happy compromise in both Raags

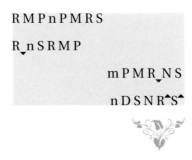

R M P n P M R S

R n S R M P

                       m P M R N S

                       n D S N R S

y spirit and I continued our aimless wanderings through India. My old age gave me the luxury of a random itinerary and I went wherever my spirit suggested I would find musical gems. I found I could meditate and find peace on remote beaches, in bland towns, in choking cities and along the banks of rivers.

I thought back on all the Raags whose acquaintance I had made, by design or by accident. Saraswati herself had created garlands from different notes and thrown them down to the earth to be discovered by Nature. How many more she must have kept to herself, I wondered. In this blink of time, my own lifetime could merely skim the surface of the vast ocean of music whose depths were unknown. I thought enviously of the stones and the air - that they did not have to worry about time and might sooner or later listen to all the music that existed.

A lifetime had passed and I thought back on all the events that I had witnessed, as dispassionately as I could. Did they really happen, I wondered. How different are they now from the dreams that came to me at nights? Who is to say what is real and what is not?

My spirit saw my brave attempts to handle nostalgia. It said nothing. It knew that I was a simpleton, gazing wide-eyed at the collage of sounds searching for meaning.

My spirit and I snuggled together in a train compartment one January. The train was moving slowly over the plains of the Ganga, in no hurry at all. My fellow passengers were fast asleep. It was bitterly cold and I huddled cosily under a thick razai.

The train seemed to slowly come to a halt. I looked outside. The train had started to cross a bridge over the Ganga and suddenly stopped. My own compartment was on the bridge, but just a little beyond the banks. I opened the window with some difficulty, trying not to make any noise that might disturb my slumbering companions.

Below flowed the majestic Ganga, timeless and almost translucent. Still falling from the knotted hair of Shiva in the Himalayas, she had travelled down the plains, maturing into a compassionate, forgiving woman.

Dawn was breaking at the rim of the river and I could see the first tentative rays peep over the horizon. Trees saluted their mother by gently bowing over the river. The first few birds had already decided to wake up and announce the freshness of a new day. The scene was tranquil. The air was cold and pure. It was perfect.

My spirit slipped outside and stretched. And a Tanpura seemed to start playing somewhere, its notes skimming the surface of the river.

To my right and about thirty feet below and twenty feet ahead, I saw the priest of a tiny temple come to the banks of this holy river. And beyond, I saw a boatman pushing his boat into the river, climb into it and slowly move with the current.

Shadaj and Shuddha Madhyam seemed to envelope the earth with their tranquillity. I took in the scene and closed my eyes to savour the moment. When I opened them, I saw the wraith of Ganga in front of me.

With a beatific smile, white jasmine in her hair and a white cotton sari that billowed gently to a breeze that I could not feel, she addressed me. My spirit had meanwhile plunged into the river and floated to her feet, looking upwards adoringly.

"Of all the Raags that are my children, Bhatiyar is my favourite", she said with an indulgent smile, her voice soft and subtle.

"The short Shadaj and long Shuddha Madhyam come together with closed eyes to worship the rising sun and me together. Pancham is the sound of gradual awakening and Shuddha Dhaivat the sound of pure devotion.

The world is asleep. But the Priest that you see there uses this time to meditate. See him, rapt in contemplation, while being in Vrikshasana, balancing on one leg while raising his hands put together in salutation. He is turned towards the sun and through his closed eyelids, he sees the tender colours of ochre from the rays. Do you hear Shadaj, Shuddha Dhaivat and Pancham? It is the sound of his faith, his morning Dhyana, as he surrenders to the Absolute.

Further beyond, the Priest's younger brother has stepped into me. I test him with my icy cold water, but his will is too strong to be deterred and he walks in till he is waist-deep. And now see him recite the Gayatri Mantra and raise me to the sun in homage of his ancestors.

Shuddha Madhyam is the sound of comfort and total peace. The sound echoes from bank to bank with its profound message of salvation.

Beyond, see the Boatman, bound to me from time immemorial. Yes, it was his ancestor who ferried Rama and his wife and brother to the other bank. I have not forgotten and will not forget. His selfless act is preserved in the upper movement, Shadaj, Shuddha Nishad, Komal Rishabh and Shadaj. Piety and simplicity ring in these notes, once again exposing their equivalence with other more esoteric knowledge in the Vedas. The devotion of the Boatman and the Priest are the same and I have blessed both.

Sing Shuddha Nishad, Shadaj, Shuddha Nishad, Shuddha Dhaivat, Pancham and Shuddha Madhyam and come to me to deliver you from the unrelenting struggle of birth and death. Yes, I shall wash your sins away with love and deliver you for the final union with the cosmic reality. That assur-

ance I give you with Shuddha Gandhar, Pancham, Shuddha Gandhar, Komal Rishabh and Shadaj.

Once again, hear Shadaj and Shuddha Madhyam slowly and with contemplation. This is the time to gracefully accept the dawn and the energy in the rays of the sun. Your time has not come when your sons will cremate you on these very banks and your ashes mixed in me as those of countless others. For now, focus your quiet mind on the Shuddha Madhyam and Shuddha Dhaivat, both clear notes, both symbolic of the morning and your journey through life. The Boatman helps you cross the river of life and I, Ganga, shall be that river if you choose, with Shuddha Nishad, Shadaj and Komal Rishabh. Even the gharials who live in my depths stop and listen gravely, quite aware of their good fortune that they must live and die within me.

The Priest is engrossed in yogic contemplation. His body is still and does not sway in the cold wind bearing my moisture. His mind does not experience currents and eddies, which I have absorbed from him. And Bhatiyar, my son, has helped him achieve his goal."

As the dawn became stronger, Ganga slowly disappeared. My spirit, clean after its dip, had come by my side and was calm, full of profound peace.

I looked outside the window. The boatman had vanished but the haunting silver sounds of Bhatiyar remained in the air. I wondered that my fellow passengers were still asleep.

The train slowly moved on. Perhaps this wonderful interlude had happened just for me, manipulated by my loving spirit.

A simple tune in Raag Bhatiyar in Jhaptaal rose to my lips.

1	2	3	4	5	6	7	8	9	10
S	M	P	D	P	M	P	G	r	S
D	N	r⌃	S⌃	N	P	G	r	r	S

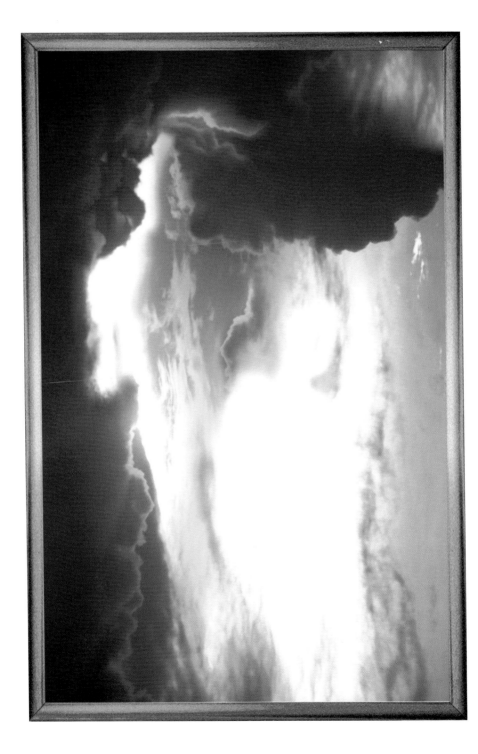

I looked back at my full life with satisfaction. Oh yes, perhaps with a few regrets, but then which life is perfect? The raw expectations in my early days of achieving fame and fortune were moderated by the passage of time with events out of my control and also of my own making.

But my greatest happiness was that I was born in this wonderful country. Yes, I was one more anonymous individual in the sea of faceless humanity of India. But so what? Take away poverty, the most venal of behaviours, suffering and more - our music more than made up for everything else! But how few knew this fact!

Maybe, as they say, music could not fill my stomach. But then, it was never intended to. It was meant to provide a reference point for me to go through life as unscathed as possible. What would my long life have been without experiencing and being touched by music? Was it mere tunes? Or something deeper? Yes, of course! The entire culture of the land was captured in the rainbow of Raags that stretched from Gujarat to Assam and from Kashmir to Rameshwaram. History, traditions, myths......great men and women had composed musical pearls and set them to Raags.

I was glad that my search for the secrets of India had pointed repeatedly at what was right under my nose. Yes, I could choose to go through life like everyone else - and to some extent I did - but having been blessed to love music, I was able to keep my sanity intact.

And now, looking back, I wondered, a little dreamily, if there was a Raag that could actually capture my life's story. True, mine was an ordinary life, full of poignancies, unfulfilled dreams, drama, the mundane, losses, relationships - no different from anyone else. So I argued logically - quite unlike me, I should add - that there must be several Raags that capture the drab, endless cycles of life.

My spirit, perched silently on my shoulder for several months, perked up. Yes, it said, I have a lovely Raag. But be warned - its undulations might cause as much pain as pleasure. Do you really want to relive your whole life?

I nodded. Yes, if I were to die tomorrow, why should I not keep all my memories close to my heart and then move on, I argued bravely. And in any case, have I not lived much longer than most?

And so, with a sigh, my spirit took to its wings and went away.

I waited expectantly. Who could it be that it would bring back? After hearing the stories of so many wonderful Raags, what could be left? I corrected myself - perhaps I had been saturated; that only reflected my own inadequacies. Greater men than I had spent entire lives feverishly uncovering pearl after pearl of only a single Raag. And here I was, asking to be satiated by dozens of them! Was I a voyeur? A musical hedonist?

And then my spirit returned with someone who looked very familiar indeed. Looking into the haze surrounding the apparition, I saw someone who I had seen before. Who was it?

It is you, whispered my spirit. And you have appeared as your memories, as Raag Jhinjhoti!

I was deeply moved. A Raag that had captured my whole life? And the

And from time to time my spirit reported back to me. It told me, in a hushed whisper, about the musical spirits behind each Raag, what they looked like and what they wanted. It described to me the emotions that each Raag had been summoned to diffuse in songs that invoked them.

I meditated. Soon I understood that the Sounds of God were in those Raags. I could listen to the sound of silence and understand the grander purpose of the Universe. Or I could listen to the Raags and let them tell me whatever they had to. It was the same. It might even be faster, not that time really mattered.

I asked my spirit to intervene. Would it, I asked, call upon the spirits of the Raags themselves to come to me and bless me? No, they would not, it said. They will not do anything for *your* ego. But ask *them* to come and ask them to reveal themselves and their purpose - now *that* was possible.

Immediately humbled, I did as advised. But first, to calm myself, I continued to meditate for several months more, letting my spirit roam free, listen and return. I listened intently to the pure sounds of the Tanpura and created the canvas within me where I wanted the Raags to reveal themselves in their complete glory.

Soon I felt like a Tanpura myself. Completely harmonized. The perfect musical construct given to help anyone who wanted to know what music and the Raags were all about. The pure notes ebbed and flowed. Adding to one another and cancelling one another too. The vibrations took their own time dying out. They were tuned beautifully. Within me.

On its own, my spirit went away one night and brought back the essence of the first Raag. Quietly, my spirit whispered the Raag's identity to me. We looked on with awe as Raag Sorathdesa took shape in front of me.

*I*n the moonlight, I saw the face of a noble, extremely intelligent and calm man take shape. His forehead was creaseless, wide and high. His eyes were calm and full of wisdom. There was deep tenderness and gentleness in them too. It was the face that came from perfect contemplation and many aeons of meditation. It knew the questions to ask God and knew what answers were likely to return. He was dressed in simple white and had a long beard. His hair was white too, but his glowing skin was so *dignified*. He was lean and sat erect and easily in the lotus position, *Padmasana*, with his hands resting in his lap. Yes, I would learn a great deal from this Raag.

Those eyes gazed at me. I looked back without fear. I saw love deep within them. As I kept looking, I saw changes in them as well. A quiet resignation, a controlled appeal, the wisdom gained from understanding the futility of existence. It was deeply moving.

As I watched, a radiant spot of light emerged from that spirit and entered me. The sounds of my Tanpura changed ever so subtly. A new note had been added. Shuddha Rishabh. Bold yet expressing itself with respect for its mother note, Shadaj, which was already present, watching benignly with a half smile.... It spoke of an awakening and told me, wordlessly, that the Sun would soon be up.

Soon other notes emerged from the spirit and entered me. A calm veiled Shuddha Gandhar came perfectly poised between Shadaj and Pancham. Soon followed Shuddha Madhyam, maternal and nurturing. Shuddha Dhaivat, brave, bold and robust, came next followed by the two sister notes, Komal and Shuddha Nishad. The elder was the emotional one, reserved and tense, who needed the younger, more expressive and gorgeous one. They held hands and moved towards me, their long hair flowing behind them and their golden saris billowing gently from an unseen breeze. This exquisite array of notes presented themselves to me. Every now and then they merged with me and exited as well. Very soon, I felt the essence of their combined message suffuse my very being. Yes, I was ready to listen to what Raag Sorathdesa had to say.

He closed his eyes and I watched. It seemed like a very long time, but I felt my limbs become very relaxed. I saw a still lake with old peepul and banyan trees all around it, their boughs dipping soundlessly in the water. In front of one tree was a very small white temple. Someone had left a few lotus flowers in front. There was no one around, no man or woman, no animal, perhaps not even an insect. But I could feel a gentle cool breeze. My mind became the lake. His soothing words drifted like feathers on the water's surface.

"Let your mind be calm and still and listen to me.

When I start, from a grave and reluctant Shuddha Gandhar, you will feel your mind being covered with a blanket of peace. This is the way you must start your quiet search for truth.

I think and I weep, that our search for the Divine starts with a question, almost a complaint. With Shuddha Madhyam, Shuddha Rishabh, then Shuddha Madhyam and Pancham, I ask for forgiveness. I know He is there and I ask with dignity what purpose is served by His not revealing Himself to me. In that simple phrase, I also answer my own question and sigh that only He knows why this is necessary, that I shall do my duty nevertheless and worship Him without expecting a reward. Can you not hear my sigh? Ah, the gleam of the majestic Pancham, shining in its lonely splendour, ringing out long like a beam of light in the pitch darkness of space...

Sing me slowly. Silence is part of me. And I will lead you to that which you seek, call it God or anything else.

Every moment that I live, I ask and beg, with Komal Nishad, Shuddha Dhaivat, Shuddha Madhyam and Pancham whoever will listen, when will it all end? With Pancham I seek the life of an ascetic tormented by the love of something or someone I cannot identify. Yet there lies the answer, not elusive any more. Contemplate the Absolute through me. Sometimes I grow bold with Shuddha Nishad; sometimes I express abject hopelessness with Komal Nishad. Then my mind settles back to the ever-present, ever-reliable Pancham, which brings me back to the focused path.

Do not show me to anyone, I am yours only when you are alone. I cannot reflect your ego and I cannot show myself unless you sing me with humility and devotion with a slow cadence. Close your eyes. And when you sing me and describe me to your mind's eye, your body retreats with respect and lets your soul feel consoled. When you wish to worship in peace, with a clear and calm mind, with no movements nearby and no sounds, call me and I shall come and help you.

How beautiful the focused, calm mind is. No thought dares disturb the mind that has found peace through singing me. The eternal truths are twined within every phrase you make and create within me and they do not see the need to hide or be elusive. Why be reborn? You can commit no evil when you sing me. Your sins melt and drip away as you go past Nishad and into the next octave, exploring, exploring, asking the same questions over and over and waiting to listen to the answers again and again because they are so clear. Your mind will dive deeper and deeper into the depths of your soul, finding more and more and yet returning effortlessly to the present, under- standing that the restlessness of the outer world is an illusion that has to be endured till your soul is ready to move on from its temporary home. Your body does not seek your attention anymore. Your mind becomes the incense for the outside world. After singing me, listen to silence and see that there was no difference after all."

Though my eyes were closed, I could soon tell that the apparition was melting away. And though my eyelids covered my eyes, tears did escape, moistening my eyelashes. And yet - and yet - my mind was at total peace. I could not have been awake and I could not have been asleep.

Somewhere in the distance, a Tabla played. Almost soundlessly and completely non-intrusively. A languorous delectable Ektaal marked time unhurriedly. From somewhere deep within my mind, a musical blessing from the apparition took form and spread through me, gently caressing each cell and binding them all lovingly in worship. The blessing allowed itself to ride on the soft rhythms of the Taal, distinct yet blended.

1	2	3	4	5	6	7	8	9	10	11	12
G	-	S	R	-	M	P	-	D	M	-	P
N	S^	n	D	-	M	P	-	-	-	-	-

It played over and over and each time I heard and understood more and more. Ah! What beauty! What divine promises of eternal peace!

The spare and sweet sounds of Raag Sorathdesa covered me with cool velvet for almost a year. I slipped back to the burden of living in the world and going through the motions of being rooted in the present. And then I would find any excuse to shut myself up and invoke the Raag, which gave me so much peace.

But then, a mysterious lone thought slipped into my mind. My spirit asked me if I wanted to meet another Raag, which had so much to say. Surely the messages of the Divine are diffused in more than one Raag, it reproached me lovingly.

As if in answer, the sounds of Raag Sorathdesa diminished and faded away ever so slowly. The cool blue of the canvas of Raags darkened imperceptibly. Something richer, perhaps of silk, and hinting at jewellery, started invading my mind. Detached, I watched my mind study this heavy and extraordinarily gentle Raag, not yet sure of what it might have to say. I had to prepare to understand. There was no other way. And soon my mind was drenched in a compassionate pool of purple ether, mysterious, magical and comforting.

And now I thought of the full moon hidden behind heavy drifting purple clouds. Stars tried to peep through strands in the clouds but their moments were only too brief. There was no breeze, but it was not unpleasant.

My spirit returned behind another, extremely respectfully. Even before this other took form for my sake, my spirit touched its feet and came back quickly to me and looked from behind my heart. There was no fear, only great respect.

A woman took shape. She seemed to be just past her prime, but her mature beauty was dazzling. Her hair was combed conservatively and she wore two diamonds in it. An intricately made gold necklace and several smaller ones adorned her neck and exquisitely made bangles rested on her wrists. The rings on her fingers were muted but clearly made of rare gems. Her silver earrings were large but not heavy. She wore a deep blue silk sari with golden borders and she sat with her left leg forward and bent and her hands clasped around her knee.

A woman with rare character and matchless beauty and dignity; she did not need any jewellery. In fact, they looked better because they had been fortunate enough to be worn by her. Yes, *they* were lucky.

She looked at me with clear and confident eyes. To see her was to see symmetry. Lovely sharp features with large black eyes that had seen every-thing worth seeing. Full lips that seemed ready to kiss a baby to nudge it past that final moment before sleep.

Her lips curved graciously in a loving smile. I almost expected her to open her arms wide, as a mother might, for me to come to her, as a son might.

And as she glowed in her maternal loveliness, it grew dark. I was not afraid because I could see her and I knew she would protect me.

The Raag crept imperceptibly under my skin. The lower Dhaivat blushed and quickly drew her veil and let her older and wiser sister, Komal Nishad, say more. Pancham placed a finger on her lips to silence her and all of them raised their arms and flew skywards to bring down a sombre Rishabh before it could reach Gandhar.

"Ah, what shall I tell you, my son? Will you understand, innocent as you are? Might it not overwhelm you? Should I not protect you from maturity and the philosophies of the old?

But no. I shall hold your hand and teach you. Because you have to grow and to protect you too much would be unwise. I shall shed tears as I see your childhood slip away and you strain to leave my protective embrace. But I shall always be there, no matter how old you become. What else is a mother for?"

She struggled to hold back her tears.

"Shuddha Rishabh, flowing majestically down from Komal Gandhar, long and languid, will always be there as a place you can return to. I do not like Time. It makes you grow up and tries cruelly to kill my memories of you as a baby, once growing in me and in my warmth and then when I fed you from my own breasts and then helped you walk. When you think of me, banish Time. I have no use for it.

Sing me at night, in a garden where I can show you the shy moon that tries to tease you, my little baby with those lovely eyes, round with fascination. Sit in the cool and slightly damp grass and smell the tired earth as it too tries to sleep.

Sing me in a lower octave. I will comfort you and calm you. Your fears vanish as Shuddha Nishad, Shadaj, Shuddha Dhaivat, Komal Nishad, Pancham and Shuddha Rishabh pull you back to my lap. Yes, I shall watch you as you try to be bold and go two steps away on your small shaky legs, trying to be brave, then giving up and hurrying back. Your confidence grows only a little at a time, but that too is too quick for me. Every time you move away, when I can no longer feel your baby skin next to mine, my heart skips a beat.

What is this world that I have brought you into? There is my love. Other children. The Sun. The Moon. Day. And Night. You will grow and grow and your soul will make you search for new experiences. There is the family you will start and your own sons and daughters. Can you, my little boy with the baby face and fat cheeks and chubby fingers, actually become a father? I laugh at the thought. And cry at the very same thought because I know it will happen. Because Time, the ghost of evil Time, has already claimed you for its own and is indifferent to my pleadings as it was to my own mother's before me. See how I sing Shuddha Gandhar, Shuddha Madhyam, Shuddha Rishabh, Komal Gandhar, Shuddha Rishabh and Shadaj, acknowledging the inevitable. Yes, the Komal Gandhar is subdued, sad that it had to remind Shuddha Gandhar that the cycle of life makes no exceptions.

In all this, I have to tell you about the God who sent you, with Shuddha Madhyam, Pancham, Shuddha Nishad, Shadaj, Shuddha Rishabh, Komal Nishad, Shuddha Dhaivat and Pancham.

I must sow the seeds of humility in your heart early on, that you use the material world merely for sustenance, never forgetting that you can take nothing away when your time comes. Can it really come, I wonder uncomprehending, even as I say these words? What savage twist of destiny and inevitable fate can already claim you for death, when your vibrant little life refreshes me and those who look upon you lovingly?

These riches that you see on me are not as they seem. They represent knowledge, justice, compassion and devotion. Unhurried. There is no destination to be reached quickly. I am your mother. I have all the time in the world for you."

Those limpid lovely eyes looked upon me with love, dignity and the promise of protection! What a strange mixture! What a glorious deep Raag! Vast and yet accessible! Not for the novice but neither for the most learned! Perhaps only for the experienced, someone who could detect its subtle contours and derive comfort. Perhaps for one who seeks a mixture of the divine and the maternal?

A soft and tender voice sang out from the heavens and the clouds thinned out in reverence. From behind the moon came the beat of Ektaal once again as a dignified woman sang, in complete control of herself, not self-conscious in the least.

1	2	3	4	5	6	7	8	9	10	11	12
R	-	-	G	-	M	R	g	R	S	-	P
N	S	R	G	M	G	R	g	R	n	-	P

ow profound these Raags are, I thought. I feel God's own breath diffused in each of them. Here some Raags like Jaijaiwanti touch your heart with feelings of deep tenderness and pure love. And there, some other Raags give you peace, silence, and the calm of a remote pond - oh, the mind expands and relaxes at the same time, supremely confident and utterly at ease. I felt that I was on the verge of something; I sensed a distant glimmering of enlightenment.

But my mischievous spirit was not done so soon. Is God not restless too, it asked? Shiva destroys in frenzy. Many Raags are derived from him. I have just the Raag for you, who will confuse you and yet make you understand much, much more than what you know.

Before I could answer, it darted away and returned. Who it brought back I could not immediately say. The cool, calm and gentle breeze suddenly gave way to unexpected gusts. Leaves about me moved about and around in random swirls. A rhythm rang out from all directions. A few deer rushed about, not in fear, but as though possessed. As though unable to control their limbs while their minds were taken over by a higher power.

Who was within this hazy cloud in front of me? He refused to sit or be still and the movements suggested someone in frenzy, possessed by devotion too powerful for his body to handle.

Ah! Jogiya! I recognized it at last, the Raag that possesses you in a wild dance of devotion. The Raag that taunts God Himself while asking to be ripped apart if that indeed would allow merging with the Absolute.

The air pulsed in a definite rhythm. I could detect the edges of an *Ektara* and a regular metallic twang.

I saw the whites of his eyes and his teeth as he grinned and laughed in a fit of ecstatic devotion. His unkempt beard, filthy clothes and long matted hair revealed how deep his indifference to himself was - he wanted to achieve something and nothing else could possibly be relevant.

"So you want to learn about me? Fool! There is nothing to learn! I want to merge with Shiva, the Destroyer! I am possessed by that desire, completely obsessed and do not have time for fools who are blind to the obvious. Who cares? I know what I want!"

It was difficult to get this spirit to speak coherently and without interruptions of his own making. But he did try, completely mad though he was.

"Ha, ha, ha! Shiva! Mahadev! Neelkanth! Take me away! Kill me! Destroy me! Soon! I am but a totally inconsequential molecule of creation, which you will vaporize anyway, so why wait? I want you! I need you!"

His deranged ranting swerved violently from one end of the spectrum to another. His voice dropped and he pleaded, almost hissing.

"Please! Please! I beg of you! Let me serve you! Let me live at your feet! Let me be touched by you and destroyed! Of what use is this existence, O Lord? I cannot bear this torture!"

But then his voice rose in volume and anger.

"What?! You do not respond?! You do not care for me?! Your silence itself mocks at me! I am the signature of the Tantrics, of the obsessed! How dare you ignore me, you filthy naked Sadhu? Do you think you are better than me because you are dirtier or more disgusting to look at than I? I have crossed the hurdles of disgust, fear and loathing and now only seek death and absorption by you, you despicable Destroyer! Why do I love you? Why do I hate you? For you I gave up everything! I ran away from home, I burnt all my possessions, I lived in cremation grounds! And you do not care!?"

He twanged the *Ektara* violently, absolutely enraged by the indifference of the elusive object of his devotion.

"I cannot be played slowly for long. Mine is a restless longing and I do not have time for meditation and intellectual gambols! In the ascendance, use Shiva's note, the extended Komal Rishabh, but skip Shuddha Gandhar, which I use a little longer in the descent. Not for me contemplation at Shuddha Madhyam! Komal Dhaivat blends well with my Ektara, don't you think? Ha, ha, ha!

What do you think of this? Komal Dhaivat, Pancham, Shuddha Madhyam, Shuddha Gandhar, Komal Rishabh and Shadaj? Play it quickly and see if you understand how miserable and mad with passion and happiness I am at the same time!

Play Komal Rishabh and Shadaj again and again! It is my attempt to capture the cosmic beat and rhythm that Shiva controls and which he unfairly denies me. I hate him! I love him! I can think of no one else but him! I know I shall trap him in Komal Rishabh and so I spend plenty of time there but he knows my game! Wait! I know his game too and shall not be fooled!

Any octave will do! I will search for him and find him! He cannot escape! Jogiya is the ultimate weapon! Shiva must rescue me and destroy me, or else I might destroy him in my impatience! Yes, I dare! I have no time for fancy thoughts like blasphemy!"

The apparition frothed in frenzy as he swayed to the *Ektara*, one moment standing still, holding his head and moaning and the next, running about screaming in hopeless despair.

"Repeat again and again, Komal Dhaivat, Pancham, Shuddha Madhyam, Shuddha Gandhar, Komal Rishabh and Shadaj! Have I not told you about this before, you fool? Quickly! Lose the concept of time! Lose yourself in a trance! This is no time for order and rules! Rules are for fools and you look like one! Asking me ridiculous questions about my purpose!"

He sang in Teentaal and ran away, the tune lingering, fading in and out as his ecstasy drove him in random directions. I watched in utter disbelief while this lovely Raag confirmed whatever he had said.

1	2	3	4	5	6	7	8	9	10	11	12	13	14	15	16
S⌃	-	D	M	R	-	S	-	R	R	M	M	P	P	D	D

he mad rhythm and challenges of Jogiya disturbed me deeply for months. The ecstasy of pure devotion, the madness, the sheer possession, the uninhibited display of the desire to sublimate into something or someone else.... it was something my intellect could not assimilate and reconcile with very easily. The message was too powerful for me to grapple with and yet, somehow, the point did come across - that someone somewhere was powerful enough to evoke such extraordinary devotion. That there was someone exalted enough to draw out such fits of passion, which proclaimed a total contempt for the illusion of existence.

It took time for my exhausted soul to sift through the apparent contradictions of love and raw energy - or was it lust? Lust for God? I was afraid of exploring this blasphemous theory but another part of me immediately understood that Jogiya was perfectly happy with contradictions and, in fact, encouraged them. Nothing was right, nothing was wrong. The Raag's impatience with the process of waiting to be absorbed into the object of its love would brook no set theory of how it ought to be done.

I became curious to know more about the source of this amazing inspiration and uninhibited display of devotion. When I had calmed down sufficiently, after another year, I summoned my spirit again and requested it to help me understand.

I had never yet seen my spirit actually hesitate to venture forth and present any Raag. But it did. Was it fear? Was it a feeling of hopeless inadequacy? I sensed a trembling uncertainty, a flash of nervousness and yet extreme excitement, as it went away and returned with the representation of Raag Bhairav.

It was just before dawn. A time like no other. Serene. Serious. A time for contemplation on the one hand and a time to appreciate my own fragility on the other.

My spirit actually hid itself behind me not even daring to peep out. It felt inadequate.

The apparition of Shiva manifested itself in front of me.

I was absolutely paralysed, unable to move or ask anything. Or to even think.

Calm, composed, with His hands folded and resting on His lap, sitting in that classic way I had always imagined Him in....the air was suddenly cold. Ganga flowed from His locks, and the crescent moon rested on Him. Beyond were the Himalayas, perhaps Mount Kailash itself, snow-white. A cobra twined itself around His neck, looking at me without emotion or opinion.

A gentle hint of a smile and eyes closed... His forehead was smooth but I could see the hint of the third eye. Here was the ultimate power across all planes and dimensions.

I felt too small to ask anything. I could barely breathe, such was my state. Who gets to see Shiva the Destroyer? Who dares ask questions about something as *trivial* as Music? And yet, when a moment later, Bhairav, the Raag, expressed itself, emerging straight from the ultimate source, I felt peace. Not the gentle loving mantle of Sorathdesa or the maternal compassion of Jaijaiwanti, but that of a solid *Answer*. Where are the words that can capture exactly what I mean?

Shiva Himself said nothing from behind the gentle cold white mist that seemed to stretch about Him for undefined distances. And yet something spoke from the same source.

"Komal Rishabh sang out, enveloping the entire Universe. Unhurried. Uninterested in extinguishing itself because of the pressure of time. For time itself could disappear with the merest suggestion from Shiva.

This note, this Komal Rishabh, is the sound of peace across the Universe.

It smiles on behalf of Shiva as it observes the chaos and destruction that shake and break apart entire galaxies to culminate in absolute soundless peace.

The lower octaves capture my essence. Komal Dhaivat is grave and prolonged, the resting staff of Shiva Himself. To the one who seeks, as yourself, Komal Dhaivat followed by Pancham vibrate with the sublime beauty of this Grandest source of music, conveying at one stroke the suggestion that existence is the merest flicker of amusement that Shiva permits Himself.

No, I do not wish to convey any hint of despondency or misery. Grasp my essence and whom I am trying to represent. Annihilation, a destruction of dimensions.... Shuddha Nishad followed by Shadaj and Komal Rishabh and then returning to Shadaj, played slowly will tell you, with grave dignity, that nothing matters. If you call peace an emotion, then that is what I wrap your mind with. But certainly not hopelessness or the utter sadness of many other less mature Raags.

Are you not comforted by this fact? Does this not strengthen you as you live life and struggle to avoid the influence of things as foolish as emotions and attachment?

Use me as a vehicle to surrender to Shiva. He will understand. Sing me and watch your ego self-destruct in shame. Nothing matters in the end. Nothing. But the attitude is one of dignified acceptance, not of pointless sadness or even immature joy. When you sing or even think of the sinking, slow movement from Komal Dhaivat, past Pancham and then stopping at

Shuddha Madhyam, Shiva himself smiles softly because He observes that you have understood the greatest and most final of truths.

Sit still and savour each note unhurriedly. Shuddha Gandhar, ever loyal and consistent, will help you reach between the magnificent notes of Komal Rishabh and Shuddha Madhyam. It is the Cobra around Shiva's neck permitting itself the unnecessary luxury of blessing you. The blue Shuddha Gandhar hints at the poison stuck in the throat of Shiva.

All Raags come from me. I permit them to exist and I finally destroy them From me springs Bhairavi, intoxicating, permitting every emotion to express itself through her. She is my mate, my Ardhangani, my half, but only because I allow her to be so. I am the ultimate expression, seeking neither approval nor even acknowledgement of my existence.

From Shiva flows all sound, that which you can hear and that which you cannot. That is why I, Bhairav, am played first, perhaps unknowingly, and my turbulent mate, Bhairavi is played last. I will let you adrift in the imaginary bliss of other Raags who owe their very existence to me.

But Bhairavi! Ah, she will be too much for you! She is the other extreme! Soaked with every possible emotion, she will bind you with her tresses and imprison you always. She is the quicksand of all musical exploration. And I can only indulge her. She is, after all, my wife and yet she exists because of me. I can control her, if I really need to, but why should I? She teases you with her playful brilliance, confusing you with the illusion of every emotion at every turn. But I am stoic. Stolid, tolerant, indifferent. And since you have asked for me, I am here.

The unhurried movement from Shuddha Nishad to Shadaj and Komal Rishabh hints at Shiva's awesome power to annihilate entire universes at will. Heaving, laborious, played at the lower octave, the sequence is strong enough to stop your heart from beating. Its echo drifts imperceptibly through the spaces between universes, informing everything and everyone in its path of their imminent destruction. Yes, the word imminent here means any time starting now. A second from now or billions of years later. Nothing will remain except Shiva, benignly presiding over a pulverized cosmic and spiritual landscape.

There is no malice, no threat, no desire to cause pain or suffering and yet it announces the end."

The apparition of the Lord of Destruction slowly dissolved. The soundless yet complete message it had given me was paralysing. So much was said. I acknowledged the hopelessness of ever trying to understand it all. My own mental constructs of how things ought to be fell apart and I saw my soul, naked and useless, in a contemplative mood. At some point, whether immediately or years in the future, it would be sucked into the final cosmic reality, the guarantee of annihilation. What sublime ecstasy!

The deep beats of a *Pakhawaj*, pulsating at an excruciatingly slow rhythm broke into my consciousness. Ah, Dhrupad! A lone musician in dark blue took shape where the previous apparition had been. Slowly strumming a Tanpura and lost in his own world, he sang to Shiva. The swirling mist responded to the beats of the invisible *Pakhawaj* as this new faceless figure sang Bhairav, in a weak attempt to pay homage to this most magnificent of the Gods. The sounds were lovely, the music haunting and the Raag deigned to be explored. With Jhaptaal, in ten beats, the singer sang unhurriedly in a deep voice.

1	2	3	4	5	6	7	8	9	10
S	d	P	P	d	M	P	M	G	r
‿N	S	r	G	M	r	-	‿d	S	-

What a remarkable way to welcome the inevitability of your own end, I thought to myself. What a wonderful Raag, holding the secrets of the Universe in seven predictable notes!

aag Bhairav was overpowering. Its strength and primordial message led me to first stand back and look upon the world around me with glazed eyes. Then I looked upon my own existence and the currents of life with something touching on amusement and, occasionally, indifference. The Raag gave me strength to carry on.

And so, for many years, I wrote and I wrote. Words flowed from my pen as I tried to cover the gamut of my experiences. I ignored my spirit deeming it unworthy of even existence. Perhaps it cowered in shame and connived with the other Raags to regain its standing in my eyes.

And one night, one lovely full-moon night, I sat at my desk, absorbed in writing about the grim futility of existence. Who would read my tome was not important to me but I was possessed and kept writing. Blue moon beams fell upon my papers and I chanced to glance up to look at the source.

Despite my recently acquired sternness and apparent disinterest in things like emotion, I could not suppress a smile as I saw the lovely, absolutely full moon. My spirit giggled and asked me, in a teasing manner, if I wanted to reclaim some joy in my life, no matter how insignificant it might be in the overall scheme of things. And, being almost naughty, it ran away and brought back someone whom I recognized immediately.

It was, in fact, the image of my daughter, Chandra, as she was in her early adolescence so many years ago!

Ah, my weak link! My daughter, now a grown woman with her own children, but once the freshest of flowers! And that is how she appeared, her image as she was then. Here she was, as a ghostly shimmering wraith, at that age between girlhood and womanhood, every father's saddest and proudest moment. And she wanted to keep both, her careless late childhood and the impatience of the young who want to grow up much too quickly.

And now she had come as the essence of Raag Chandrakauns! Was this one of her pranks?

I watched with a smile as my daughter's ghostly likeness explained very seriously to me, her morbid father, why she was who she was. Her skin was smooth, glowing with youth but the beauty that she was destined to be was already apparent. How aptly had I named her! She was as lovely as the moon, as radiant! And she wore what seemed to be a sari made of blue moon beams!

I felt a touch of paternal concern to see her bare arms exposed to the cold night air but knew better than to express myself ; I knew my obstinate daughter's ways.

My spirit, suddenly in an excellent mood, sat by me smiling as my daughter explained Raag Chandrakauns!

A luxurious tapestry from the Tanpura was laid out, with the very important absence of Pancham, replaced by Shuddha Madhyam. Once again a reminder of the mischievous character of my daughter, who always wanted to do things differently, provided, of course, that I was around as a safe anchor! Incidents from her childhood flashed across my mind's eye and I fought hard to blink away the tears that accompanied my smile.

"My dear Father! How wonderful you were to me! I could not have asked for anyone better under whose love I could grow up! Always pretending to be strict, yet perfectly happy to let me finally have my own way! I knew that you knew, and yet I daringly took advantage!

This Raag, this lovely thrilling Raag, is played in the middle and upper octaves. Restless, joyful, bright and gay, it will lift your tired spirit and re-kindle the appreciation of beauty. And how could it not? It is Shuddha Nishad that does the magic! As Bhairavi was the tree where Bhairav was the deepest root, I too, as this Raag, am the flower growing on the branch of Malkauns. Komal Gandhar, Shuddha Madhyam and Komal Dhaivat hint at Malkauns and the magic is Shuddha Nishad, breaking away from serious thought and allowing you to enjoy beauty and gaiety without feeling guilty!

Come Father! Do not be glum! Look out of the window and see the moon! It loves to be admired! It loves to be told that it is beautiful! And so it is with me! Even if you have a heart of stone, it will melt and rise upwards to show itself as a smile on your face! The movement of joy is in the quick Komal Gandhar, Shuddha Madhyam, Komal Dhaivat and Shuddha Nishad.

Why be weighed down by serious thoughts? If indeed our existence is futile, as you feel, why not go through it with a smile? Try to sing me, dear Father, and see the moonbeams light up your heart with no effort at all! But sing me at night when you can see the Moon too. The Moon will laugh and blush that it is being admired and you can tease it and praise it even further. Sing in the upper octave: Komal Gandhar, Shuddha Madhyam, Komal Gandhar and Shadaj and watch the Moon embarrassed by your lavish praise of its beauty."

My daughter's lovely black eyes twinkled as she laughed.

"Oh my serious Father! Forever pretending to be preoccupied by weighty matters! You never minded when I pulled your hair and ran away! You scolded me when I would chatter away into the night and disturbed your sleep in the next room, as I pretended to talk to the moon, my friend. But do you know? Perhaps that was why I was able to become one with the Raag of the Full Moon, Chandrakauns.

Shuddha Nishad! Oh, what a splendid note! It rides on every moonbeam, falling on the face of one who fell asleep waiting for it, and slipping away naughtily from one who kept awake! But you can always catch it; it is not a firefly that tries to run away from the clutching hands of little children fascinated by the light. Komal Gandhar represents perhaps you, Father. A little sober, a little dignified. And it all falls apart by the piroutte of the cheerful Shuddha Nishad as it skips gaily through the Garden of Raags, stopping here to admire and smell a flower, stopping elsewhere to gaze at a butterfly and then looking back and calling out impatiently to the other notes, especially Komal Gandhar to hurry up!

And, do you want to know a little secret? Well, I shall not wait for an answer, as I need to keep talking! Every now and then, almost without warning, you ought to try singing Shuddha Rishabh especially in the highest octave! It will ring out unexpectedly, almost as the Moon suddenly emerges from the clouds, playing a game of hide and seek.

Am I not beautiful, Father? Your precious gem, your lovely Chandra, always lightening your heart as the full moon lights up the night. I am the nightingale of the night, sing me often, never forgetting to repeat Shuddha Nishad as often as you want."

And my daughter's image ran away, laughing happily as I gazed out of the window at the dead of night, my hands on the window sill, and felt a huge lump growing in my throat. I felt a strange sense of deja-vu. I remembered how I had once cried, many years ago, about how she would soon be gone to another, more distant age, where I, her Father, would have lesser meaning.

Which is perhaps why Chandrakauns is always short and sweet, because the most beautiful of things do not last.

The moon shone and I heard my daughter sing a simple and bright tune in *her* Raag, in Teentaal.

1	2	3	4	5	6	7	8	9	10	11	12	13	14	15	16
											S$^\blacktriangle$	-	d	-	N
S$^\blacktriangle$	-	-	-	NS$^\blacktriangle$	Nd	M	gM	g	S	-	NS$^\blacktriangle$	-	d	-	N

hough I had slipped into a state of melancholy for a while because of seeing my daughter's image from a bygone time, Chandrakauns had served its purpose. I developed a more positive attitude and looked forward to more light-hearted and playful Raags. Why be bogged down with grim thoughts when I could let my soul bask in warm sunlight and happiness? I smiled and laughed at the most absurd things and found joy in all manner of vibrant life.

My spirit saw this change in me and was happy as well. "Ah, there are so many Raags with plenty of restless energy! They tease, they laugh, and they raise your spirits. Wait, I shall be back with a very special one, because I like to see you like this."

And it darted away with a laugh. It came back in a moment. All I could hear was laughter and high-spirited shouts. This time my spirit did not come right back next to me. It danced with whomever it had brought and played, as it never had before. And this time, what took indistinct shape was a garden in spring with several young girls playing and shouting excitedly! This was the essence of Raag Kamod.

My impish spirit refused to return and I sat and watched fondly as it played cheerfully with its new companions!

"Happiness! Irrational joy! We celebrate the energy given to us and praise God! We do not know what sadness means! We dart here and there, playing hide and seek with each other, and laughing out loudly and without care!

I, this collective I, am Raag Kamod. Restless, happy, flushed with the absolute joy of being able to experience life!

Sing me, and your life will be full of gaiety. The women inside me giggle and whisper secrets to their friends. Did we, indeed, emerge from the time when Krishna played with his Gopis? Each Gopi sought to do more to get a second of his attention. Each smiled and showed her pearl-white teeth and blushed when Krishna happened to tear his eyes away from Radha and saw her. What gay, tremulous, fleeting romance!

The flowers in the garden themselves bloom quicker and force out colours from themselves that they never felt necessary to before. The birds dash through the air in wild abandon, singing their most precious and personal tunes. This is the beauty of me, Raag Kamod!

Where in other Raags, Teevra Madhyam seems strained and reserved, here it encourages the celebration of life. But where would it be without the light blue sparkling Pancham? The movement is never straight! A few notes up and then a few notes back, refusing to conform to order! With cheeks flushed and forehead perspiring, call out Shuddha Gandhar, Teevra Madhyam, Pancham, Shuddha Gandhar, Shuddha Madhyam, Shadaj, Shuddha Rishabh and Shadaj and tease the young newborn fawn who just peeped from behind the Peepul tree, curious to know what the fuss is all about! And it will come straight to you without fear because it knows it can celebrate its new life without inhibition!

A Koel calls out repeatedly, Shuddha Madhyam, Shuddha Rishabh, Pancham! Sitting on the bough of a flowering tree, it cocks its head to one side and curiously watches the scene below as young girls play Dandiya with sticks, their bright red ghagras and green cholis sparkling with bits of mirrors! With their hair flying behind them, pairs of girls hold hands and twirl, laughing with excitement. One or two are exhausted and they lie panting on their backs on the lush green grass, their young breasts heaving, still laughing. Bold yellow butterflies flit from the flowers near them and sit right on the tips *of their noses and the girls do not wave them away but instead pretend to talk to them! Everyone teases everyone else with love! In the midst of all this is the source of all excitement and love, Krishna himself, playing me on the flute! I am Kamod, created by Krishna in celebration of nature and life!*

Teevra Madhyam, Pancham, Shuddha Dhaivat and Pancham! How well this jasmine string of notes radiates happy restlessness when sung quickly!

Explore me in the upper octave, full-throated and without restraint. Shadaj, Shuddha Nishad, Shuddha Rishabh, Shadaj, Shuddha Dhaivat, Pancham - these are the birds in the garden calling out urgently to Krishna asking him to take note of them too! And he smiles and looks at them lovingly, acknowledging them with the notes Shuddha Gandhar, Shuddha Madhyam, Pancham, Shuddha Gandhar, Shuddha Madhyam, Shadaj, Shuddha Rishabh and Shadaj. With a thrill of pleasure, the birds take to the air and now try to retain his attention by darting up and down, their bodies etched against a bright blue sky, preening and showing off their uninhibited flying.

I do not have time any more to talk because I must go and join everyone else who dances and sings with innocence and joy and pure love!"

So saying, Kamod went away, moving hither and thither, spreading laughter and smiles for all to grab and taste. I wondered if I had actually seen Krishna in the midst of the mad swirl, full of lovely young girls in their flush of youth, playing and creating games and doing all they could to attract his attention!

I had to call out to my spirit to return, which it did, flushed with the perspiration and joy of having expended energy. It still hummed.

M R P!! m P D P G M R S

G M P G M S R S!

N S⌃ R⌃ S⌃ N P m P   G M P G M S R S

G M R S, G M P G M S R S!

A squirrel peeped in through the window to inquire if it could share in this joy! Could I possibly say no?

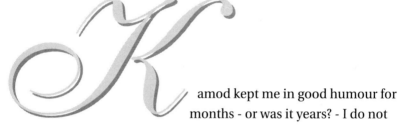

amod kept me in good humour for months - or was it years? - I do not know how time sped by. For me, every season was Spring and everywhere I saw visions of Krishna with a mischievous smile, a peacock feather on his head, playing the flute surrounded by birds and animals and lovely Gopis. I danced in colour, in bright lights and capricious breezes. I enjoyed life.

But sooner or later, the vagaries of life's experiences pulled me away from Kamod's hypnotizing, almost narcotic effect. I could not stay immune to the human experiences of loss and grief, though I tried to be a philosopher. It did not matter that I was past the age of sixty; the passing of one near and dear, the realization that he would never come back - it was too much to bear though I had been through similar loss before. And the suffering of someone else with a disease that knew no cure. What could Raag Kamod do here except momentarily cheer me up?

I pondered on why we are given life at all. With suffering all around me, and my sheer inability to do anything to banish pain from the hearts of all those I loved, I wondered what the purpose of creation was. Is life only about suffering, interrupted by interludes of joyful experiences?

My spirit watched me with concern as it saw me being threatened by deep depression and hopelessness. It thought deeply of which Raag to bring that could comfort me while understanding my plight as no one else could.

Much before dawn, I had woken up. The night was still deep and dignified in its blackness and showed no signs of ever relinquishing its hold on earth's mantle. My eyes were closed, wet with remembering innocuous events connected with those whose presence I would never know again. And through the film of tears, I saw the emergence of the Lord of Creation, Brahma.

My spirit nestled in my lap as I saw the apparition and wondered how to react. Ah, so Raag Charukesi had decided to come to me, its essence speaking of Brahma himself. I did wonder if this might not be a contradiction, but who was I to question?

I bowed in salutation and the apparition smiled in loving benediction. With eyes soft and all knowing, compassion streamed forth as soft red light. Sombre, and soaked in the knowledge of the transient joy of creation, which would inevitably end, it sought to comfort me with answers. Behind him was the vision of Saraswati, the Goddess of Knowledge, for whom music is the most sacred of chapters.

I heard the sound of a Tanpura. Each vibration arose from nothing, lived fully for the briefest of moments and then slowly melted away. From the apparition, seated on a lotus, came a dulcet ever-vibrating Komal Dhaivat in the lower octave. At once dignified, commiserating and respectful of the privacy of grief, the note did not try to comfort, merely to acknowledge my pain. Shuddha Rishabh, still and serene, evoking thoughts of a landscape of silence caressed my moist eyes. But it was the Shuddha Gandhar that completely mirrored my questions. It did not seek to provide any answers; it sought to confirm and repeat my pain.

The four-headed Brahma sat on a Lotus whose pink petals shone with iridescent dew. His white beard and compassionate eyes told me how much of misery he had seen.

"Charukesi. Yes, it is I. With the promise of creation and the warning of the accompanying pain of existence that you will experience.

I was born from the navel of Vishnu with the task of creation. A task that seemed joyful at first. But the consequence of death, over which I have no control, causes me to wonder why I should preside so majestically over countless births and creations.

Spend time at Shadaj, lovely as the lotus you see, arising from the middle of the lake of sorrow and pain. The pain you feel is the prelude to another creation. I will send back the one who has gone from your life. But alas, not as the one that you hope for.

Komal Dhaivat in the lower octave too broods, melancholic, accepting the inevitable and resenting the experience of a heavy heart.

Be lifted up by Komal Nishad, travel past Shadaj and Shuddha Rishabh to rest at Shuddha Gandhar, the purest of notes, perfectly balanced between Shadaj and Pancham. In this note is distilled your pain in the most beautiful form. Though you sing it and your tears well up and burst out, you cannot move away from it because this is the note that truly reflects what you feel.

Pancham is an admonition to me, the one who created, perhaps recklessly, without thinking of the consequences and the suffering of one who must live on without those they dearly love.

The sequence of Komal Dhaivat, Komal Nishad, Komal Dhaivat and Pancham is the gentle caress of understanding. Useless words of comfort are not necessary at this time. At this darkest hour before dawn, it acknowledges your pain and does not try to diminish it.

Sing Komal Dhaivat, Komal Nishad, Shadaj, Komal Dhaivat, Pancham and Shuddha Madhyam and the grief that makes you want to end your own life will be expressed. Yes, I shall bear the burden of the pain you wish to express.

Do you see a woman on the verge of death, her hair carelessly spread across the pillow as she gives up the battle after having just created a new life? How unjust are the Gods, giving from one hand while taking away with another!

Komal Dhaivat, Komal Nishad, Shuddha Rishabh and a long languid Shadaj once again question the reason for existence, knowing that every answer is meaningless. Your cry of pain, that you thought was stuck in your throat for so many days, has already travelled the galaxy seeking justice for this absolutely unfair event. But what can I do, what can I do? I am cursed to create!"

Did I see Brahma himself shed a tear that he was unable to stop creating and perpetuating the pain of existence? Saraswati touched his upper arm gently in understanding.

And through Charukesi she spoke.

"All knowledge resides in this Raag through my grace. I too am Charukesi. Those who sing this because it completely understands grief also find consolation and a spiritual maturing. See Pancham, Komal Dhaivat, Komal Nishad, Komal Dhaivat and Pancham come together and compassionately try to answer your fevered questions. They tell you that existence can continue in your memories of the departed. As they lived, they transferred some part of themselves to you in your memory, so that you could remember them when they are gone.

Yes, I am Pathos. Deep and grave and yet fragile as a new butterfly, I, Charukesi, shall lead you past the painful joy of creation. Sing me before dawn, when the night is the darkest and the stars are the only witness of your grief-stricken mind. Sombre, serious and deep and yet so beautiful, I am the Raag through which you ask for a reason for the pain of existence that you had no hand in."

Saraswati led Brahma away gently into the sky. She turned and looked at me with sweet compassionate eyes. My grief had not diminished but I knew I was not alone.

From the eastern sky, the sun asked to be allowed to diffuse light into the blackness. From her Veena, I heard a lovely tune in Raag Charukesi.

1	2	3	4	5	6	7	8	9	10	11	12	13	14	15	16
											R	G	M	-	d
P	-	-	-	R	-	G	M	R	-	S	R	G	M	-	d
											S	-	d	n	d
P	-	-	-	M	P	d	n	R	-	S	S	-	d	n	d

I wept unashamedly.

fter my daughter's teasing through the dazzling Raag Chandrakauns, and then the incredibly moving Charukesi, I recovered my sense of balance for a while. But I lost myself in thought again. The reality of existence has been forced on me, I thought. It was senseless to simply withdraw from this gift of life. If I did not choose to enjoy the illusionary pleasures of life, should I not find another way to tolerate it?

Perhaps the Yogis have already found the answers, I thought. The Karma Yogis work and are yet detached. Those who practise Hatha Yoga keep their gross body in good health to facilitate a more efficient attainment of the Lord. They live in the dissonance of life and the inevitability of death

My spirit watched my thoughts take shape and slipped away. When it came back, it came back not with one spectre but several. An ensemble, in fact.

I saw the Golden Temple in Amritsar in the fog of the early morning in December. Indifferent to the bitter cold, a group of Ragis, musical priests, sang Shabads beautifully in the open courtyard. Dressed in pure white, with deep blue turbans, with flowing beards and eyes closed, they sang the praises of their Gurus and spoke of their teachings. They did not address me and, in fact, I could not hear anything distinctly except the essence of the Raag.

The Tabla kept pace gravely without embellishment. The oldest Ragi, sang with the feeling of one who completely understood the deepest essence of the Raag after years of singing. The others who accompanied him were dignified and respectful, using their vehicle of devotion with care.

Ramkali. Oh, what a lovely Raag! Rare, fragile and strong, the perfect vehicle to lose oneself in the Lord.

And so a calm voice said:

"I too have come from Bhairav.

I know that everything will end, but the gift of life must be respected. Your experience must be clean, sinless and pure.

What are these men saying? Their message is to ask you to step away from attachment while being rooted to the world. Watch your parents age, watch your children go, watch wealth appear and disappear. Never feel sad about these things but participate nevertheless, because to be detached from those who too must exist for no fault of theirs is to be a coward.

Through me, you will achieve Ram, the Lord of the Worlds. He will reside in your hearts and guide you through this existence. The harsh word evaporates even before it forms in your mind. Violence transforms to gentleness and love. Lies disappear and humility reigns. Hate will have no meaning and revenge will seem pointless. You will see the Lord in the poor and the sick and will serve them without any expectation of reward or recognition. This is the beautiful purity of me, ancient Ramkali.

In the early morning, just after dawn, the devout stir to begin the day. I express myself at this time, a gentle reminder to all that each day should be spent in acts of devotion and piety. Teevra Madhyam, used sparingly, pushes Pancham and then Komal Dhaivat to seek the feet of Komal Nishad before returning to Pancham through Komal Dhaivat. This magical sequence alone shows the way.

The white purity of this Raag softens the heart of the most wicked and guides him to the nearest Gurdwara where he seeks atonement falling at the altar of the Guru Granth Sahib. The Guru blesses him and wipes away his sins that he may escape the cycle of death and birth.

Teevra Madhyam, used sparingly, is the only loving admonition to the straying devotee that you will hear. For the one who covets the temporal and the gross, I only ask that you listen to me in the middle octave as I ascend as in Bhairav and deviate from it in the descent with the necklace of musical pearls, Teevra Madhyam, Pancham, Komal Dhaivat and Komal Nishad. But the path resumes again and I do not linger at Komal Nishad, returning to Shadaj through Pancham, Shuddha Madhyam, Shuddha Gandhar and Komal Rishabh. Do you understand now the secret within me? Do you understand now why the Yogis spend all their time seeking me out? I have the simple answers for their ultimate release from the bondage of birth and death. Like a bud about to bloom in the early morning, I too offer the path to salvation, to the lotus feet of Ram.

Lust, avarice, and attachment - all diminish and finally vanish by singing me. Yes, the Lord has wished me to help those who want to learn how to live a clean and honourable life, in anonymity and service, with chaste deeds and total humility. That is I, Ramkali."

I felt myself in the midst of these wonderful humble musicians as they advised the world through this enchanting rare Raag. Unlike the frenzy of Jogiya or the subliminal message of destruction in Bhairav, this Raag spoke of a way of life that accepted reality solemnly.

1	2	3	4	5	6	7	8	9	10	11	12	13	14	15	16
d	-	P	-	M	P	G	M	d	P	m	P	Dn	d	-	P

The morning had matured and the devout, streaming into the Gurdwara past these wise musicians lost in the still rapture of Ramkali, resolved to live simply and humbly. And I turned away from the slowly dissolving vision with head bowed, ashamed of every act of selfishness that I had committed, and seeking to find God through the message of this beautiful Raag.

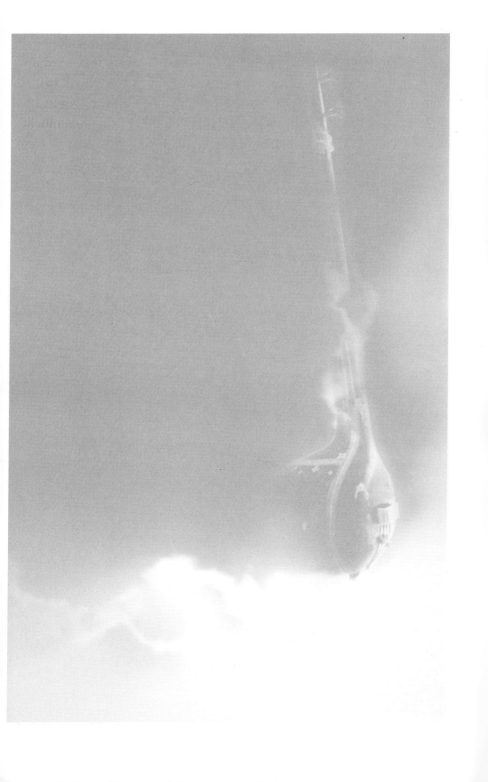

hich Raag is the most Majestic, I asked my secretive spirit. Which Raag is the most regal, the grandest? Who gave us Chandrakauns? I must know!

Chandrakauns was light-hearted and thrilling but just as the tendrils of the creeper enjoy themselves in the air while clinging on to the banyan, so too must there be a Raag that benignly permits innocent laughter while keeping unknown deep secrets to itself. That is what I demanded of my spirit.

Let us wait once again for the deep night, it replied. Wait for the night of the new moon when all is black as ink and every soul chooses to rest. Then I shall bring you who you want to meet.

I waited impatiently for the moon to wane. The half moon became a quarter and then a mere sliver. And finally, it cloaked itself demurely in black.

My spirit darted away and returned with a dignity I had not seen it display before. With it was something distinctly regal, distinctly ponderous and deep.

In spite of myself, I stood up and bowed with respect and reverence. I just knew that respect was due; respect was this Raag's right to demand.

In the blackness of night, the air still and the trees asleep, with animals resting to begin another day of fated existence, an apparition took shape. With a simple silk sash across his dark muscular body, and with eyes grave and all knowing, Raag Malkauns stood before me, his right hand raised in divine benediction.

"Are you ready to hear my message?" he asked in a deep resonant voice that travelled to the ends of the Universe.

"I give the knowledge within me to only the true seeker, one without ego, one who can handle me with respect since I will never belong to him. I can be yours briefly only when you fall at my feet and do not dare to look up and see my face. For my face has seen all existence, in the past and future. I am the King of Raags, Malkauns. I cannot be treated trivially. No one is ever ready for me.

Yes, I gave Raag Chandrakauns permission to exist as a benevolent ruler allows his subjects illusory freedoms.

From my throne, Komal Dhaivat in the lower octave, I look upon the supplicants who come with heads bowed and hands folded in reverence. My power spreads across all the octaves and all the other notes shrivel and shrink away, to revive only when I move on.

Komal Nishad is my counterpoint, the seat of my minister, who advises me on matters of state. Always loyal, always mindful of who I am, it speaks when allowed and always lets Komal Dhaivat preside and decide. I do not permit Pancham lest the light-hearted note diminish in any way the sanctity of my celestial court.

Komal Gandhar is soft and sweet, occasionally adding mellowness and reason to me. Of what use is a Monarch who cannot discriminate wisely and allow kindness and mercy to exist alongside the administering of discipline?

Komal Dhaivat is acknowledged even without singing it. All the other notes revolve around Komal Dhaivat, just as the planets revolve around the sun. Sing Komal Gandhar, Shuddha Madhyam, Komal Gandhar and Shadaj and understand the great truth in the unsung note Komal Dhaivat.

I rule over the emotions. I cause the deepest and gravest feelings to swirl slowly around you, just as the Milky Way with millions of stars moves imperceptibly around a central point.

Komal Dhaivat gives peace, calm and order to the troubled turbulent mind. The movement between notes is slow and gradual, like an elephant bearing me as I survey my Kingdom of lesser Raags. Each note blends into the next without breaking. All that I do must show reason. Nothing capricious can exist when I am sung.

Sing every note slowly and peacefully. All manner of existence come to me with their own tale of sorrow or joy and all are consumed within me. And so to one I can appear to describe the flowers in a garden. To another I seem to describe Nataraj performing his shattering Tandav Nritya. To yet another, I describe the beauty of the night. I am mature, all knowing, suffused in wisdom from aeons past.

Why do I mesmerize you? Perhaps because of the way I carry myself with extreme dignity, borne on the shoulders of notes and Raags who cannot match my power and dark brilliance.

When I am sung, all that came before me and all that will come later will appear mere shadows undetectable in the darkness of night.

By merely singing me, your own questions will seem small and petty, unworthy of being asked in my Divine Court.

Come to me and let me bless you. Come to me for divine justice. Come to me to see me sift through truths till I help you find the final, most valuable one."

So saying, the apparition of this regal Raag, seemed to sit on a throne made of the darkest of nights and ascended slowly upwards, melting away while I kept my head bent and hands clasped in supplication.

What a wonderful majestic Raag, I marvelled. The King, the Emperor, the Ruler of the lesser Raags. A mere half note away from joyous frivolity, keeping its balance soberly and declaring its infinite celestial superiority through restraint and with powerful swathes between notes...

From an unknown source deep in the recesses of the night came the sound of a Rudra Veena. Malkauns in a slow Teentaal, establishing its majesty and authority over and over.

1	2	3	4	5	6	7	8	9	10	11	12	13	14	15	16
								g	M	g	S	‚n	S	‚d	‚n
S	-	-	-	‚n	‚d	‚n	S								

he deep and grand Raags of the night possess a haunting magic all their own. What makes them so special, I wondered? As the sun tires of his task and all living forms prepare to recoup for the next day's struggle to survive, the night Raags soothe in a different way. Their notes warm those shivering under thin blankets. They make men dwell on the deeds of the day past. They make the pious marvel that they had the chance to see another example of the relentless passage of time, the greatest sign of God himself.

But while most slipped into the comfort of dreamless sleep, I was awake. I reflected on all the Raags I had met and whose blessings I had sought. In the glimmering of the twinkling stars acknowledging me from aeons away, I walked slowly on a lonely road, far from habitation, far from the tumult of hysterical civilization, where no one had the time to even breathe. The net of total illusion, Maya, had been cast and all were trapped. I dared struggle, because I was now old and could afford to.

I felt the wrinkled skin on my hands without feeling sad. But memories of a time when I was young and never imagined that I would age, kept coming back. My beautiful young wife, my innocent cherubic children - all had been tarred with the brush of time. I did not resent it, as I had been blessed by the knowledge of the divine from other Raags.

Who should I meet, I wondered, who could explain Time? Who had understood Time and could explain it to me, of limited intellect and poor spiritual insight?

My spirit looked at me askance. Can you really handle the Raag who has the answer? Understanding time is not for an emotional man like you, it said.

I shall try, I answered. And if I fail, I shall try again when I am reborn. Again and again.

And so my spirit went away, with a shake of its head, and returned with Raag Puriyadhanashri. And since it wanted to see what I would, it sat softly on my eyelashes, perhaps to confirm that it had seen exactly what I would.

A slowly swirling, luminescent helix stretched infinitely in both directions. Moving imperceptibly but surely, both light and darkness emerged from this astral wonder. I saw yawning space, I saw light being formed, I saw gases liquefy. I saw heat captured in ice.

I saw the Gods themselves step back in awe from this wonder that they had created and which in turn had created them.

"Surrender completely to me," said this indescribable apparition. *"I am formless, faceless. No one can capture me, no one can control me. My shadow falls on everything and everyone and escape is impossible. I have watched the Universe from when it was the tiniest speck of dust.*

My Teevra Madhyam is unlike any other. Power vibrates from it and subdues all other sound. From this note follows Komal Rishabh and Shuddha Gandhar, spanning the physical world. All nebulas are trapped within the grip of this grave combination. Komal Dhaivat and Pancham played in sequence without any hurry carry the ponderous weight of my truth. It is the question that you ask and simultaneously the answer.

I move neither forward nor backwards as the rest of you trapped in my relentless current. If it is night on this earth, it is day elsewhere. I shall witness countless births and deaths but shall not grieve. I shall witness beauty and sordid decay but shall not be moved by either.

The lower octave begins the process of blessing you with the gift of time that you may see change and be enchanted by it. Teevra Madhyam, Komal Dhaivat and Pancham cloak the entire universe with my inescapable essence. None may flee from it.

Through Shuddha Nishad, Shadaj and Komal Rishabh in the higher scale, I ask you to surrender to me gracefully and with dignity.

Sing Shuddha Nishad, Komal Dhaivat and Pancham and feel your own sorrow at being unable to control me. But I seek no excitement and I have no ego and therefore resent nothing. It is my duty to control you and finally consume you.

Shuddha Nishad, Komal Rishabh, Shuddha Gandhar, Teevra Madhyam, Shuddha Nishad, Komal Dhaivat and Pancham! Ah, from end to end across all dimensions, they proclaim my grandeur and mastery over all.

Shuddha Gandhar, grave and dignified, blesses you with restraint.

Only at night do you see my beauty because when night arrives, you realize that time has passed. Play me unhurriedly. Play me carefully and with infinite patience. My power is too much for the weak to handle. I soak invisibly into your consciousness, completely mesmerizing you with what I have to say. Desperate to halt the passage of time, you grieve for more to experience. But that is not mine to grant. And even so, I shall consume you in the end. You are nothing. You have been touched by me and are helpless.

Your hair greys and your skin withers. Panic is useless. You grieve for a lost moment, you long for the smile of your lover. But nothing endures but me and I cannot be reversed. Sing me and enjoy my notes so that I can treat you with affection."

So saying, the ghostly wonder retreated. I saw planets, I saw energy, I saw many nothings. And I saw its supreme power as its grave and wonderful notes affirmed, once again, that only Time could exist without a break.

And without any accompanying rhythm, these notes settled around me, as though from nowhere.

m r G   r S   ₋N r G m P   N r⌃ N d P   d P̣ d m r G   r S   m r G

hough Raag Puriyadhanashri was powerful beyond description, Kamod kept creeping back into me. Was it my mischievous spirit, defiantly loyal, wanting me to be light at heart? I kept seeing visions of the Gopis dancing for Krishna's attention. Their passion for the Lord was a delight to behold. Their innocence carelessly threw aside any suggestion of philosophy and sober thought. The yellow tinge in the images drew me to the enchanting worship of Krishna.

Finally I gave in. I longed to see whom it was that the Gopis were jealous of. No matter how he looked at them, no matter how the twinkle in his eye seemed intended only for *her*, every Gopi knew to whom he had truly given his heart. They could never match her. She possessed him and he possessed her. For fleeting moments each Gopi felt Krishna had a soft corner just for her, but in the heart of hearts she knew it was hopeless. This woman, Radha, was the one for whom he lifted his flute to his lips and played his divine tunes.

Radha - a woman just like the others, but clearly much, much more. A woman whose fervent love for Krishna was returned in equal measure. How wonderful must such a woman be, I thought. Of the earth of Vrindavan and of the golden dust of the heavens. What passion she had, what love! And how fortunate she was!

My spirit watched me, bemused. It had never thought it possible for a man like me to think of women in this manner. Mothers, daughters, wives - yes. But as the lover of the Divine? How improbable!

But I was not to be discouraged and I ordered it to bring to me the Raag that would contain the essence of Radha. And it flew away to Mathura, to Vrindavan, to the banks of the Yamuna and asked the soil, the grass and the water for whatever hazy memories they still had of this woman who had captivated Vishnu's avatar.

It did not have to look long. Her image was still fresh and nothing that had seen her or heard her voice was willing to ever let that memory fade. And when my spirit came back, it brought with it a living painting of a scene on the banks of the Yamuna.

I bent forward, curious. I saw the afternoon sun beating down upon the banks of the river. And under a solitary tree, I found Radha.

A plaintive Shuddha Madhyam slowly sank into a Shuddha Gandhar. Here was Gaur Sarang, trying to explain to me Radha's plight.

"See Radha leaning against a tree on the banks of this holy river, sister of Ganga. Her eyes sad and drenched with tears, she looks at the clear blue sky, unseeing.

He had promised to come. He had promised to slip away from his gang of cowherds and come unseen to meet her at this lonely spot that only the two of them knew about. The very earth and the trees were sworn to secrecy He had promised to come, hold her hand and play the flute just for her.

And she had run away from her friends, her curious teasing friends, who knew exactly what was going on. They were jealous but they were equally proud. That one of them was Krishna's lover. That one of them had his love. Through her they could feel his love for them too, though perhaps not to the same extent as Radha.

She had run in the hot sun, her hair flying behind her as she skipped over stones and the hot baked earth towards the shimmering silver of the Yamuna. To the lone tree that knew her and welcomed her.

And he was not there. She had waited and waited. But he had not come. He had not kept his word.

See how Shuddha Gandhar, Shuddha Rishabh, Shuddha Madhyam and Shuddha Gandhar, played slowly and lovingly, seem to catch the very pulse of Radha's sorrow, her betrayal. Shuddha Madhyam is her soundless cry of indescribable sorrow. And Shuddha Gandhar holds Shuddha Madhyam's hands and consoles her. Did you tell him about the exact spot? Was this it? Could it have been that tree, just beyond that rising earth over there? Or could it have been at a different time in the evening, at sunset?

No, Radha shakes her head. Shuddha Nishad, Shuddha Dhaivat and Pancham in the lower octave proclaim her absolute surety - yes, I am sure. When we came to the Yamuna in the early morning with the cows and calves, we whispered to each other about the spot and the time and we pointed at this very tree. There was no mistake.

Pancham, Shuddha Rishabh and Shadaj. No, she shakes her head, regaining her composure and confidence. He will certainly come. Perhaps he could not tear himself away from the cows he loved. She smiles as she wonders if perhaps he is still trying to steal one last scoop of butter from the mud pot dangling high above from the ceiling in Yashoda's kitchen. She would wait a while longer.

The hot sun sneaks through the green leaves waving above her head. It too wants to look at this lovely Gopi. But the leaves will have none of that and shut the sun out again. They are selfish and want Radha all to themselves. They sway, creating a cool breeze for her. But it has no effect, for her sorrow is deep.

Teevra Madhyam, Pancham, Shuddha Madhyam and Shuddha Gandhar is her heart-rending cry for justice, her appeal to Krishna to come to her as he had promised. Pancham, Shadaj, Shuddha Nishad, Shuddha Rishabh and Shadaj is the expression of her apology to Krishna for anything she may have said that offended him. Should love not overlook her careless words, meant to tease, but that have perhaps hurt?

A white dove flies down to the lap of the sitting Radha, her head on one bent knee and her face tear-stained. With her lovely liquid eyes she looks at this heavenly consolation and takes it in her cupped hands.

Will you be my messenger, she asks. Will you go and tell my Krishna to come? Whisper Shuddha Nishad, Shadaj, Shuddha Dhaivat, Pancham, Shuddha Madhyam and Shuddha Gandhar to him, lost as he must be, playing some reckless dangerous game with his uncouth friends, and he will remember that we were to meet. Go lovely bird, go and tell him of my love!

The leaves in the tree are themselves moved by her plight. Can you not hear them sing Teevra Madhyam, Pancham, Shuddha Dhaivat, Shadaj, Shuddha Dhaivat, Pancham, Shuddha Madhyam and Shuddha Gandhar? They tell Radha that Krishna does love her that she should not doubt him and he would surely come. And then would he not be disappointed to see her in this condition, with red eyes and stained face?"

This hauntingly beautiful Raag mesmerized me. Love for the divine was in each note and the sequences were touching. I felt a touch of anger towards Krishna that he had betrayed Radha and caused the birth of this profoundly tender Raag.

And as the painting dissolved, it left its notes behind as a parting gift. Radha herself sang

> G R M - G
>
> m P D S⁺ D P m P M G
>
> G R M - G P R S ˎN R S G -
>
> G R M - G

I longed to sit by the Yamuna, my feet dangling in its waters, as Radha must have done while she waited and waited for Krishna.

houghts of the agony of Radha filled me with righteous indignation. Why should I be respectful of Krishna, I asked angrily. Such pure love, such earthly innocence - how dare he subject such an Apsara to such agonies?

How humiliated she must have felt, how betrayed! Who was this pretender who claimed to be God and saw no crime in dishonouring the object of his love by not meeting her as promised? What would she say to her friends, who would cruelly mock at her? Would they not say that Krishna was not worth her love? And that he did not love her?

My spirit saw my helpless anger, the anger of an old emotional man, and laughed. All this is part of a divine plan, it said. Why do you feel the story is over? Do you care to know what happened next? How can the Lord in Krishna's avatar betray such love?

But which Raag would know what really happened, I asked in some agony. All I can imagine is that Radha suffered humiliation and Krishna did not care at all!

My wise spirit slipped away quietly and eagerly. It was night, with a moon that seemed to say that it was there only for lovers to get inspiration and yield to their passions, perhaps in tears of pure joy.

The air was suddenly thick with the sweet smell of Mogra. I was once again on the banks of the Yamuna. The moon's reflection broke and merged again and again in the delicate ripples of the gently flowing river. And I saw Krishna's Radha standing by the banks. But she was not alone.

With eyes closed and her head tilting back on his shoulders, she rested in the dark arms of Krishna himself. His cheek was on her head and his eyes were open, limpid with compassion and gentle understanding. His arms were around her waist. He smiled as he took in the trembling rapture of Radha, who held his forearm, scarcely believing her fortune.

A very different Shuddha Dhaivat enveloped me. At once deep and melancholic, it left my knees feeling weak. I sat down, knowing I was in the presence of the most romantic and erotic of Raags, Bageshree. It was this very scene, which proclaimed itself as the essence of Bageshree.

"How lovely it is to behold such tenderness! The pure heart of Radha filled with love and devotion for one whom she calls her lover and whom she knows is someone much, much more. To be made love to by the Lord of the Universe himself....to be touched and caressed by Krishna himself. Who can describe such ecstasy?

I am Bageshree, the Raag of Love", said a soundless voice of honey from this picture.

"My Lord, Radha asks, I waited for you. Why did you take so long? Can you not hear her say this with Komal Nishad and Shuddha Dhaivat blending into each other?

His fingers slowly travel from her shoulders along her arms to her fingers, slowly and tenderly, apologizing soundlessly for his unintended slight. Was he not here now? Was this not the best time after all? When none but the Moon can see them and when the Yamuna itself has stopped to catch a glimpse of her beauty? And the Moon has hidden herself with a veil of clouds because she dares not be seen when a lovelier woman turns her face upwards, softly lighting the skies with the glow of her desires?

His warm breath falls on her neck and she shivers with indescribable emotions, unable to understand what is taking over her body. Shadaj, Komal Gandhar, Shuddha Madhyam, and Shuddha Dhaivat express her emotions like none other. And the lovely resting at Komal Gandhar gliding down from Shuddha Madhyam is her sigh of satisfaction that here, now, her lover was none other than Krishna himself.

Shuddha Madhyam, Komal Gandhar, Shuddha Rishabh and Shuddha Madhyam ask on Radha's behalf, for the briefest of moments, if Krishna is sure that they are not watched. Who could come this far to this remote neck of the river at this hour of night, he questions her lovingly and reproachfully. Then we shall make love, she says, her fears allayed, stilling her suddenly beating heart. And she says this with Shuddha Madhyam, Pancham, Shuddha Dhaivat, Komal Gandhar, Shuddha Rishabh and Shadaj.

He takes out his flute to play for her. No, she says, gently pulling away his divine instrument, you have played the flute for me so many times. This time, I shall sing for you. And she raises her face to the moon again, with a wonderful smile, unable to contain her happiness. Look how she expresses herself with Komal Gandhar, Shuddha Madhyam, Shuddha Dhaivat, Komal Nishad and Shadaj. This Shadaj echoes sweetly through the Galaxy.

Krishna holds her lovely face in his cupped hands. She cannot breathe and she cannot but close her eyes. She feels his sweet breath on her eyelashes and then she feels him gently kiss her moist lips. She opens her eyes, trembling, wondering what she will see. She looks straight into his eyes, barely away. Their eyelashes mingle and with her eyes, she sees not his black irises but the entire Universe.

Shuddha Madhyam, Komal Gandhar, Shuddha Rishabh and Shadaj in the upper octave capture her understanding of what she has seen. Stars, moons, planets, time. For she has looked into the eyes of God himself and cannot believe what she has seen.

Shuddha Dhaivat, Komal Nishad and Shuddha Dhaivat - she sings to ask, to confirm, is it really you?

And with the drooping Komal Gandhar, she answers her own question for the thousandth time. I have come and will never leave you again. And Radha believes him, yes; never again will you be out of my sight. How well she says it in the haunting sequence, Shuddha Madhyam, Komal Gandhar, Shuddha Rishabh, Shadaj, Shuddha Rishabh, Komal Nishad and Shuddha Dhaivat.

Hold my hands, O Krishna, and let the tips of my fingers touch yours! Do you know what pain I suffered because you did not come when you said you would?

Her reproach is soaked in Shuddha Dhaivat, Komal Nishad, Shadaj, Komal Nishad and Shuddha Dhaivat.

Yes, he says, I am guilty, through Shuddha Madhyam, Pancham, Shuddha Dhaivat, Komal Gandhar, Shuddha Rishabh and Shadaj. Punish me later, but let me now feel your hair with my fingers and feel your soft cheeks with my own.

With Shuddha Dhaivat, Komal Nishad, Pancham, Shuddha Dhaivat, Komal Nishad and Shuddha Dhaivat, he whispers into her hair. We are one, are we not, he asks. You do not even know who you are, none other than my Divine Consort, and our love is in each cell of creation."

The tender scene evaporated slowly, and I found my eyes wet with tears as sobs of pure joy shook me apart. The Moon seemed to know what I was feeling. And the smell of Mogra remained after the apparition of Raag Bageshree had vanished.

D n P D n D....M

M P D... g R S

D n S⁺ M⁺ g⁺ R⁺ S⁺

g⁺ R⁺ n D ...... n D M....

M P D... g R S

My spirit lay absolutely still, immobilized by this sweetest and most poignant of Raags, containing more feeling than any living being could possibly express.

The haunting sweet fragrance of Bageshree drove me to distraction. From morning till night I was swayed by its exquisite power. I could not sleep, crying out without warning as a particular musical movement came into my consciousness from no-where. And to be awake was to live in a state of resentment, that I was forced to stay away from the intoxication of this unbelievably emotional Raag.

It seemed as though the fruits of months, if not years, of stern medita-tion and self-control had been reduced to waste by a single Raag.

My hitherto active spirit too was in a state of stupor. It reflected me but was - presumably - previously wiser. But now, after hearing Bageshree, I could see that it was finding it difficult to find merit in any other Raag.

But with an effort, I tried to regain my composure. I resolved to resume my search. Having no commitments that needed my attention, I travelled alone across India without a plan, staring out at the landscape, from the window of many trains. I saw beauty in the seething humanity in railway stations. I saw dignity in the filthy streets of towns that I passed by. And the lush green fields with no man in sight moved me. My fellow passengers, stepping in briefly from the mist of anonymity, spending time with me silently in a compartment and then departing, never to be seen again - I wondered about their experiences in life and the significance of the paths of our lives crossing, albeit for only hours. How must they have regarded me - an old man lost in thought, talking to himself, perhaps shedding a tear at irregular intervals.

Soon, it seemed that I had recovered. I plunged back into deeply philosophical thoughts and the clack-clack of the trains seemed to provide the reference meter.

But Alas! All was undone the moment I accidentally woke up in the late evening after a nap and found that the train had arrived in Mathura on the very day of Krishna Janmashtami!

There was a divine reason for this extraordinary coincidence, I felt, especially after my insights into Kamod, Gaur Sarang and Bageshree, and I promptly, without further internal debate, picked up my little suitcase and stepped off the train.

I walked uncomprehendingly past porters and hawkers and out of the station. I kept walking, ignoring everyone.

I knew that my spirit too was awake and would guide me.

After several hours of aimless walking, I was outside Mathura, being drawn by some unseen magnet that wished to complete another Chapter of the Tales of Krishna. In the night, I could smell the heady lingering mix of water and the light of sunset and I knew I was on the banks of the Yamuna again.

I sat on the banks at a remote spot. Three young women passed by with their cows and calves. The bells on the necks of their cows and the silver anklets on the bare feet of the women jingled together. They passed by, perhaps wondering about the strange sight of an old man, an outsider, sitting alone on the banks of the river that was their life.

Why are we here, I asked my spirit? I thought I would not let the Raags born from this holy place torment us? I search for peace and detachment but how will I find it here where the very air whispers the names of Radha and Krishna?

But drunk on the tranquil beauty of the place, and listening to the echoes of the music that must have drenched this place for thousands of years, my spirit did not answer, but simply floated away.

I looked across the silver and black Yamuna. On the other bank, I saw a cowherd walking back to his village with his cattle. Fireflies briefly lit up the weeds along both banks. The birds had long since returned to their nests.

Suddenly, I heard the sound of a Tanpura. I turned and saw that my spirit had returned with someone. Why, it was the very same group of girls who had passed by me earlier! They glowed in the dark and their feet were not on the ground. And with them were the lovely cows, eyes large and limpid, full of love.

I splashed my face with the cool water of the Yamuna, but they did not disappear. My spirit dived into the river and from there, listened and watched the three Gopis.

"We, the three of us, are the essence of Raag Patdip", their silver voices declared. *"Born of our love for Krishna, our Gopala, Patdip speaks of not only Radha and Krishna but us as well. We were of no less importance!*

After an exhausting day's work, we, the Gopis of Vrindavan returned from the fields and meadows with our cows and calves. Like every day, the soft glow of the oil lamps in the windows of our huts beckoned to us. Though our limbs were tired, we were still excited because we knew that we would now have Krishna all to ourselves!

In his divine love, Gopala never rejected any of us and gave all of us the same love and attention. And his magic was such that he was with all of us at exactly the same time, his blue limbs and peacock feather equally real to all. And he would play the flute for each of us while we lay down in the sweet-smelling hay in the cowshed with our heads on his lap, chewing a strand of grass and then sharing it with the calf that came to be touched by Krishna.

Though we were but ordinary girls of this village of Yadavas, Krishna gave us the same love that he gave to Radha and the same that he gives to those who worship him.

We never forgave him for stealing our clothes on the riverbanks and humiliating us but his charm and his flute allowed us to enjoy his divine presence every night."

And as two of them turned away to tend to their beautiful cows, the third continued, lost in romantic memories brought alive by Patdip.

"Shuddha Nishad is my plaintive cry to Krishna asking that he stay with me a while longer. Am I not equally lovely, I ask him with Shuddha Nishad, Shadaj, Komal Gandhar, Shuddha Rishabh and Shadaj, why go elsewhere, when I am here for you?

Outside the first sprinkles of rain threaten to snuff out the light from the oil lamp on the window. Let it, for let not even the night look inside and see me in your arms. How can it be possible, as they all say, that you are everywhere at exactly the same moment? You are here now, and I can smell the fragrance of your cows on your limbs. Are you not playing the flute just for me?

No Krishna, do not hold my wrist and pull me away with you to the woods for your dance in the moonlight. I shall come if you dance only for me. With Shuddha Madhyam, Komal Gandhar, Shuddha Rishabh and Shadaj, I ask my own Krishna to reserve all his time and music just for me.

Krishna assures me with Komal Gandhar, Shuddha Madhyam, Pancham and Shuddha Nishad that his Lila is only for me and I hold his hand and we run out together, believing ourselves unobserved. And at exactly the same time, Krishna does the same thing with all the other Gopis!

In a clearing in the nearby forest, I see Krishna with the moon as his halo. He takes up his flute and closes his eyes and plays. The cows and calves too have come, refusing to be tied down, with their ropes miraculously having come undone. The rest of the village sleeps in spite of the tinkle of so many bells, and I have Krishna only to myself. How can I believe you when you say Krishna enacted this scene for all of us? I was there and he was there too! I saw no one else!

I sigh with Komal Gandhar, the sound of contentment and welcome my youngest calf into my lap with Shuddha Madhyam and Pancham as we watch Krishna play while the forest dances to his wondrous rhythm. The flowers that were to bloom only at dawn simply could not wait and have burst forth, releasing their aromas into the night air and filling me with longing, even though the object of my love is right in front of me! I shake my head and sing Shuddha Dhaivat, Shuddha Nishad, Shadaj, Shuddha Dhaivat and Pancham to confirm that I am not dreaming!

Krishna raises me to my feet and wordlessly asks me to dance too! But I cannot, so overwhelmed am I by the moment. The calf nudges me on and I finally, tentatively, move my feet to his tune. I place my small pale hand, trembling and nervous, in his dark strong one and he tightens his hold on me, reassuring me that he will always be there for me. With the Shuddha Nishad again, long and prolonged, with Shadaj, Komal Gandhar, Shuddha Rishabh and Shadaj, he asks me to trust him and have faith. And that is when I close my eyes and place my head with my eyes closed on his blue chest, my body wracked with sobs of sheer joy. And he comforts me, knowing how much I love him, with Shuddha Madhyam, Komal Gandhar, Shuddha Madhyam, Komal Gandhar, Shuddha Rishabh and Shadaj.

He did the same thing to all of us! We guarded this most private of secrets believing ourselves to be Krishna's only one. But when we found out he had done the same thing to all of us, we were not jealous or amazed. We were even happier!"

As the trio, three sisters tied in love, disappeared, someone played Ektaal on the tabla, from the depths of the river Yamuna. A lone flute seemed to play from the darkness of the woods on the other bank.

1	2	3	4	5	6	7	8	9	10	11	12
N	-	S˄	D	-	P	M	-	P	g	-	M
g	-	S	g	M	P	M	g	S	R	-	S
S	Ṇ	S	M	g	M	P	M	P	N	-	S˄
N	S˄	g˄	R˄	-	S˄	N	-	S˄	d	M	P

I walked slowly back, tearless but thankful to know the origins of this tender Raag.

hough I never lost any opportunity to slide into the heavenly joy of Raags like Bageshree and Kamod, I did not forget the majestic grandeur of Raags like Bhairav and Puriyadhanashri either. I knew that the final message was in the convergence of the mysteries of all these. Then again, perhaps there was no final message. Perhaps the search was its own reward.

Declaring myself incompetent to fully appreciate subtle nuances in various Raags - leaving them for the analysis of Pandits with much greater knowledge - I resolved to continue my research for own satisfaction. At my age at that time- I was in my seventies - time never seemed enough to close unresolved issues. There was enough time, of course, for regrets, but luckily, my desire to use Raags as a means to prepare myself for the end helped me shrug away morbid and oftentimes wasted melancholy.

The vicissitudes of life had snapped any ambition for personal glory and the need for recognition. I was happiest with my grandchildren, and when they ran away from me, I let them go with pride. I felt I continued in them and I recognized uneasily that this meant that my ever-present ego was still alive and well.

I went on a pilgrimage - as all old people do who wish to close their final chapter by suddenly becoming pious - to Mansarovar. It happened to be a very good time to go, in early April, with Spring in its full glory. Along the way, with my fellow travellers, we saw fields upon fields of lush meadows with wide swathes of colour; flowers of all types were in full bloom.

We took care not to pick any flower, merely admiring them. Shiva beckoned us urgently and my frail legs tried to keep up with those younger and more impatient.

And one afternoon, we camped in an open field completely drenched in flowers. At a distance, snow-capped Mount Kailash was visible, standing in benign splendour and presiding over this vivid display of new life.

I asked to be excused, and my spirit and I walked away, taking in the heady smells and soft rainbows all around us. The buzzing of bees, the mad chirping of birds, the smell of fresh earth vibrating with new life, the dance of eagles high up in the sky - I looked upon all this with wonder. Had I become so lost in dour matters of philosophy that I had forgotten how to enjoy myself - to feel, to touch, to smell?

My spirit held my hand and bade me lie down on a bed of delicate flowers. Reluctantly, I did as asked, fearing that I might, a mere human being, destroy a far more wonderful example of God's creation. From my position on a slight knoll, I could still see the abode of Shiva. Butterflies with fantastic patterns on their paper wings flitted about, perhaps unaware of their part in this ethereal Plan.

I was in front of Shiva himself, standing with Parvati. Once again, I saw that benign smile, but this time of indulgence - as he looked upon the restless gyrations of his son, Ganesha, perhaps as a three-year-old boy. He wore a small white dhoti, tied up at his pot-bellied waist. His trunk waved above him, sniffing restlessly at all that was in the air. His little tusks were intact, perhaps because he had not yet grown up to the age when he would snap off half of one of them to write the Mahabharata for Vyasa.

I held out my arms tentatively, and Ganesha ran away from his protective father and fearlessly jumped into them. And it was not to find contentment, most certainly. He pointed to a field of flowers that he wanted me to take him to. I looked at the divine couple for permission and they nodded, with half smiles.

The little boy in my arms could not stay still! I was too slow for him! I tried to walk fast to where he wanted to go, but he was impatient and jumped off onto the ground, and ran towards a huge bed of lush flowers, shouting with joy. Concerned that I should not abdicate the responsibility given to me, a mere mortal, by Shiva and Parvati, I called out to him feebly.

But should I have worried at all? I soon found him sitting in the midst of a gaggle of baby birds and animals, holding forth solemnly on a new game of hide and seek he had invented. Everyone dashed off in random directions! And hid themselves while Ganesha counted till ten, pretending to cover his eyes, while secretly peeking from an opening! He ran after a fawn, he jumped up at a young bird; he blew cheekily at bees that were busy at work; he tugged the tail of a rabbit with his trunk, he threatened to pluck off a feather from the tail of a peacock! No one was safe from him, yet everyone seemed thrilled to have this young God in their midst, for his merest touch guaranteed salvation.

Who was this little boy, this little God with powers beyond comprehension, I wondered? And my spirit whispered with delight, he is the meaning of Raag Basant.

As I watched the young Ganesha gambol in the fields of flowers, cheerfully shouting out at the animals, at the sky, at the sun, at the wind, at the Universe itself perhaps, I heard a Tanpura blend itself seamlessly with this wondrous scene.

The spirit of the Raag spoke, from the constantly moving baby God, who from time to time would teasingly throw a shower of flowers in my direction.

"Life begins in spring time, when all is new and full of energy. It is the time to dance and sway to the tunes of nature. There is no colour that is out of place, no flower that is disallowed. Animals have given birth, and the

83

babies of all creation look around them with wonder and innocence in their eyes! They dance to any rhythm, create music out of the petals of flowers that have bloomed in abandon and profusion!

The sparkling stream over there tumbles and shouts aloud, asking everyone to jump into it! Insects visit flowers everywhere and the Gods themselves smile with amazement to see the vibrant life in their creations.

Men and women play Holi, vainly trying to imitate nature, and everyone's thoughts turn to love and bright feelings. All wish to create and dance! I am the spirit of Raag Basant.

And this is the time to pray to Ganesha, whose benedictions at the beginning of every activity are so important. Light-hearted and yet all-knowing, he can be played with, loved, scolded - which other God permits such liberties so innocently?

As you watch him gambol through the meadows, a little God with all knowledge, sing the notes, Komal Dhaivat, Shadaj, Shuddha Nishad, Komal Dhaivat and Pancham in the upper octave! This is my signature, the signature of Spring!

Birds fly down and sit on his large ears, teasing him. He uses his trunk to try to catch them, but he lets them get away and then follows pretending to seek revenge. He slips and tumbles and gets up on his own, his knees muddy, but chortling nevertheless!

Teevra Madhyam, Pancham, Teevra Madhyam, Shuddha Gandhar and then Teevra Madhyam and Shuddha Gandhar speak of the beauty of creation at this time of the year! In the nests, the most innocent open their beaks asking to be fed constantly and the parents rush about in the sky searching for food! See the fish in the gurgling brook jump out of the river trying to catch the sun! This is the time for the brave and the innocent, for lovers and those who nurture! Understand this in Shuddha Gandhar, Teevra Madhyam, Shuddha Nishad, Komal Dhaivat followed by Teevra Madhyam and Shuddha Gandhar.

And while Ganesha bends at the stream and uses his little trunk to suck up all the water, if not the Universe, to let it go a moment later, you are reminded of his magnificence through Shuddha Gandhar, Teevra Madhyam, Komal Dhaivat, Shuddha Gandhar, Teevra Madhyam, Shuddha Gandhar, Komal Rishabh and Shadaj. This lovely garland helps you understand that Ganesha indulges in the joys of creation for a reason he hides from those who enjoy the moment. This is no time for reflections - only pure, thrilling joy!

But hear the wisdom of Ganesha in Shadaj and Shuddha Madhyam. He knows what the others do not know and do not care to. He knows that there is more to this than creation. There is wisdom in the notes, but the young think of it as another little game of fun. This reminder is brief and almost undetectable before you hear the slow sliding ascent to Teevra Madhyam returning to Shuddha Gandhar, proclaiming the beauty of life.

Ah, Ganesha finally rests! He sits down on the grass and allows the fawn to come and lick him! He swats her away affectionately after putting some red, white and purple flowers in her ears and looks about for a ball! Finding none, he raises his trunk and sucks down the protesting, struggling moon to rest at the end of his trunk. Then he throws it up and down in delight, frightening the rest of creation! He threatens to jump into the sky and rearrange all the planets as per his whims! They appeal to his parents to save them from this naughty child! For all the young in the galaxy, this is a fun-filled game in which they want to participate!

Did you detect a shade of Puriyadhanashri somewhere? How can such a light-hearted Raag contain the accent of a far more serious one? But such are the contradictions that Ganesha indulges in for the joyful young!

I move quickly, always sliding away from you, playing, teasing. I am the easiest to enjoy but the toughest to handle because I am restless and not interested in discipline! And why should you expect such a thing from small children? Let them enjoy themselves without inhibition, doing whatever comes to mind!"

Ganesha was called away by a Koel calling him repeatedly with a high Komal Rishabh and Shadaj. Had he gambolled for far too long? Would his parents be worried, I wondered?

My spirit asked incredulously who was innocent? Ganesha or I?

But I picked up the squirming youngster, who pulled at my hair with his trunk! Braving his antics, I nevertheless took him to his parents and placed him at their feet. After which I fell at the feet of this child, for I knew his awesome power.

I awoke abruptly. Was it a dream? There was no Shiva, no Parvati and certainly no Ganesha anywhere around. In the distance, Mount Kailash continued waiting impassively for me. But only inches away, staring at me wide eyed, was a fawn with red, white and purple flowers in its ears! I sang out aloud, my heart bursting with joy!

> d S⁺ N d P,   m P m G m.... G
>
> G m N d m G,
>
> G m d G m G r S
>
> S M...., m M G,   m D N S⁺ R⁺ S⁺

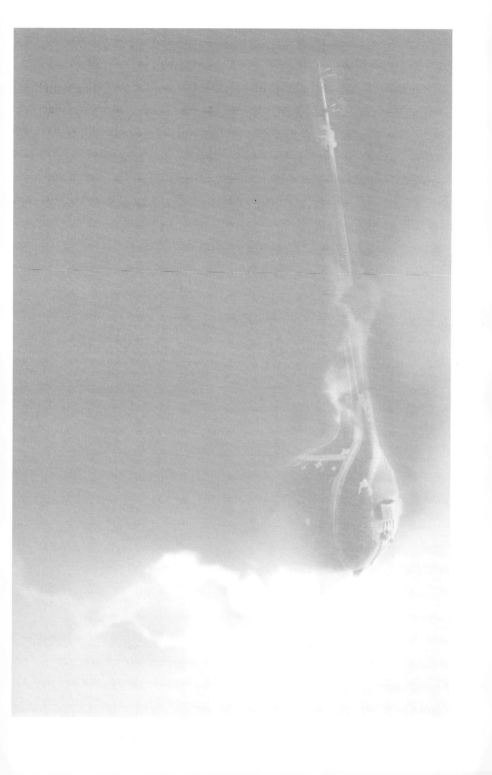

ring me the Raags of the countryside, I demanded of my spirit! All the Raags I have met have been wonderful, no doubt, and capture my country's heartbeat beautifully. But what do the people in the countryside sing? So lost must they be in the struggle for existence, that deep philosophy, poignancies and celestial currents must not have any meaning.

Old Man, you are arrogant, rebuked my spirit. Just because you have not heard them does not mean that the Raags of the countryside and of the vast rural lands do have not have grave meanings. Indeed, our music is rooted there, not in the cerebral walls of Pandits hiding from the battles of life.

You are right, I said, chastened. I had thought that my capacity to withstand the emotional onslaughts of wondrous Raags had been reached, but my spirit's mysterious veiled hint ignited my interest. I called upon my spirit, in utmost humility, to bring one such Raag.

To which my spirit, with a smile and a twirl, disappeared and returned with what I could only call emotion. I could see the shimmering sands of Rajasthan, the Rann of Kutch, villages near Banaras, the rice fields of Bengal and Assam. On and on the kaleidoscope went, each more poignant than the next. This was my India, where I was born and where I hoped to die.

Finally I settled on the visage of a woman from Mewar. With heavy silver anklets and a colourful dupatta with lovely beadwork and embroidery draped over her head, she stared out at me with large black eyes, holding a pot on her hip.

My spirit came and sat by me and bade me show the respect that was due. I got up and then prostrated to this humble illiterate village woman in whose music was more practical wisdom than those combined in several thick volumes written by Vedic scholars.

The apparition seemed to reach down and lift me up. Then she pulled her veil across her lovely face. I saw that her skin was weathered by hard work, the soles of her feet were cracked from wear and her hands were rough from unrelenting labour.

Then she said, *"Simple to write down and impossible to play without understanding me, I am Raag Mand.*

In every village of this ancient land, where there is a river nearby or where there is no watering well for ten miles, you will find me. When people stop work and mark the happy events of life or when they merely search for a way to bear the grinding monotony of everyday life, I am there.

I am simple and unlettered, but soaked in me is the origin of thousands of Raags. Each lilt, each curve in each tune that uses me shows a willing acceptance of destiny instead of hopeless depression. We have no time to indulge our emotions except when we rest after back-breaking work.

See how the Shuddha Swars convey strength and resilience and a cheerful willingness to navigate through life without questioning.

Play me at weddings, at births, whenever the ancient temple seven miles away by the dry riverbed celebrates a festival. Play me when the harvest finishes. Play me on your instrument and smell the hot dust of Mewar. Sing me and feel the celebrating of the people of Ayodhya when Rama's birth was announced. Or hum me and be transported to when Krishna wed Rukmini and the people of Dwarka knew no limits to joy.

Always ascending with confidence, the string Shadaj, Shuddha Gandhar, Shuddha Madhyam, Pancham, Shuddha Dhaivat and Shadaj is like the thrill of the village women as they gather to dance in the clearing in the middle of the village.

With simple eight-beat and six-beat rhythms, and simple two lines that say everything that needs to be said, I make sure that people remember me.

Shuddha Gandhar, Shuddha Madhyam, Shuddha Rishabh, Shadaj allow you to use me to describe another joyous event. Yes, perhaps it is that your daughter has given birth to another pearl. Or perhaps your son's engagement to the lovely girl in the next village has been announced.

You accept the congratulations of your friends and family, gathered on this occasion, with Shadaj, Shuddha Gandhar, Shuddha Madhyam and Pancham, and then Shuddha Dhaivat, Shuddha Nishad, Shuddha Dhaivat and Pancham. God has been kind again.

With tunes that use me, little known legends of this area are preserved forever. Did you know, for instance, that when Krishna travelled from Mathura to Dwarka, he rested at that temple along that road? Did you know he blessed our ancestors and said he would always remain in that temple and allow them - and now us - to worship him? No, our stories are not complicated, but are as intense as yours and very important to us.

When the village barber takes out his drum and beats it, the men gather and repeat the ancient stories of their heroic ancestors who helped Rama on his way to Lanka. I lend myself to these people, the real holders of the heritage of this land called India.

Sleep with the warm cows around you and sing me. They know me. Yes, they know me when their keeper hums Shuddha Gandhar, Shuddha Madhyam, Shuddha Rishabh and Shadaj. He asks his peaceful cows questions and answers them himself with a tuneful, Shuddha Nishad, Shadaj and Shuddha Dhaivat and Pancham.

These celebrations are short. They reaffirm relationships, they bind them, they create new ones - all the while holding on to a way of life that has come down through centuries. When the men of our land went to fight wars as soldiers for Kings they had never seen, we prayed for them and welcomed them back with tunes composed in me. When the rains came and the first tender shoots of sugarcane poked inquiringly through the soil searching for the sun, I was there. I am Raag Mand, the Raag of Mother Earth."

With a lilting Pancham, Shuddha Dhaivat, Shuddha Nishad, Shadaj, Shuddha Dhaivat and Pancham on her full lips, she lifted her pot to the top of her head and walked away to the fields to continue her interrupted chores.

I stared after the departing woman, completely humbled, electrified by the experience of meeting this soft and expressive rustic Raag.

My spirit and I sang

S G G M P D, N S[⌃] D P........G M R S

as we watched the sun dip and disappear.

y experience with Raag Mand had chastened me. Gone were any hidden lofty pretensions of somehow being privy to great timeless secrets. The same seven notes that spanned the heavens vibrated with the earthy scents of mundane existence - and made it look beautiful! The Raags of nature, I mused, were perhaps tied to time and events on earth. But that did not make them any less profound.

I asked my spirit once again. The elements of earth must have inspired such poetry and such wonderful music. Who best represents heat? Cold? Water?

My spirit answered testily. There is no Raag that contains every single secret, though all may hint at the existence of another. Do not ask for too much, I have already shown you enough!

Outside the hot summer sun beat down on all of us. The earth was parched and cracked. Even dust had no energy to swirl around and make our lives miserable. It was just too hot to even step outside. The air was still; even it was exhausted by the relentless heat. The rivers were dry; the fish themselves struggled to live. Animals tried, as best as they could, to protect their young ones from the cruel sun by searching for shade given lovingly by trees that sought nothing in return.

I lay limp, soaking in perspiration, too drained to even think, let alone indulge in romantic fantasies about Raags and other esoteric subjects.

My spirit watched me thus and slipped away on the shoulders of a current of hot air. I did not notice it leave and could have done nothing in any case. My eyes were swollen.

But suddenly, I smelt something different! Yes, it was the smell of the dry earth just after it received rain! Indescribable, incomparable! I looked outside, but there was nothing. No cloud broke the monotony of the brilliant blue sky. I shaded my eyes with my hand and searched but there was nothing, absolutely nothing. There were no clouds, and the heat continued to sear everything it touched without mercy.

From my bed, I saw my spirit re-enter the room with a dark cloud. They stopped at the foot of my bed and I propped myself up to see this vision. Already I felt cool!

The cloud cleared only partly to reveal the torso of a dark, handsome and muscular man. He looked at me fearlessly. On his wrists were bracelets made of small black clouds, rotating constantly. From his eyes and chest flew small sharp bolts of lightning. Rolls of muted thunder filled the room.

This was Raag Megh, waiting for the right moment to attack the heat and replace it with its own benevolence.

For the first time, I made bold to directly address the spirit of a Raag. I am weak with exhaustion, completely fatigued, I said feebly. The heat does not let me even think. I beg you, I pray to you, please do something!

"Sing me and I shall gladly help", said this ghostly wonder in a deep echoing voice that seemed like thunder.

"Collecting water from across the land and from seas, rivers and ponds,

thick clouds roll across this, your land, waiting to shower it with its treasures. The heat retreats upon seeing me, inflicting its last cruelties on the helpless earth.

The deep slowly rolling Komal Nishad, rising from Shuddha Dhaivat, is the announcement of my presence. Sing it and clouds will form, catching the wisps of water that had no place to go. Slowly, water comes together, understanding its purpose. The clouds darken little by little. They block out the sun and fill the skies. Light cannot penetrate the thick layers of black clouds, immensely strong and powerful, gathering force. Hanuman blows upon them gently pushing them in the direction where they are needed the most.

Soon the shadows caused by the sun seem to disappear, for now the shadows are those of the clouds themselves.

In the lower octave, Komal Nishad moves unhurriedly, hinting at awesome power as the clouds gather and become pregnant with more water than they can hold. Pancham is the sound of patience, for those who need water are beside themselves with grief at the delay. And so I must be sung without unseemly haste.

Honour my dignity by not making me too dependent on time. I shall fulfil the promise within.

Women and children excitedly rush outside their homes to look skyward and welcome the dark clouds in the distance! Can the long summer finally, actually, be about to end?! No one can believe it! Peacocks dance in mad excitement and they sing me! Shuddha Rishabh, Shuddha Madhyam, Pancham, Shuddha Madhyam and Shuddha Rishabh, they go on and on whirling and announcing the beginning of the monsoon.

And the clouds benignly and boldly roll into each other, filling the sky with crashing thunder and flashes of lightning! Shuddha Dhaivat, sparingly used, is the transient fear that those feel when they hear these loud noises coming unexpectedly from the skies. Quickly forgotten, Pancham and the deep sonorous Komal Nishad continue the proclamation of this, the happiest of times.

And soon, the first drop falls on the face of the new baby whose father has taken it out of the house and raised it in the air to be blessed by the clouds!

There is laughter everywhere and the grim seriousness of all living things is miraculously washed away as more drops form and fall on the parched earth!

The drizzle becomes a torrent and everyone dances in the rain, throwing aside all inhibitions! Birds do not seek shelter but dance instead. Calves frolic in the rain, unable to understand why they are so happy, and not caring either!

I am the Raag that calls upon water to revive life. I am the Raag that challenges heat!

The farmers breathe a sigh of relief. Their crops will survive. For the children, this is the time to jump naked into the nearest pond and look skyward laughing and shouting as the rain pours down harder and harder on their upturned faces!

Flashes of lightning add to the festive joy of the moment. Claps of thunder snuff out all other sound. Little children clutch their doting, laughing parents in fear and soon realize that they should be wildly happy instead.

Nature itself sings me. Komal Nishad, Shadaj, Komal Nishad, Pancham, Shuddha Madhyam, Komal Nishad and Shuddha Rishabh. The clouds bow in homage to me, the only power they know that can control them. I watch proudly from the heavens as heat evaporates like the water it had similarly wounded!

Now water collects, forming streams and rivulets. The dry riverbeds come to life and soon the river forms, slowly yet surely. It regains its beauty and gushes madly with joy, cleaning away dust and grime. There is water now, enough for several months. And where there is water, there is life! Sit by the banks of the river and sing me, Raag Megh!"

The apparition rose and moved towards the window and moved into the sky. I had not even noticed, but it was raining outside! My hopelessness vanished and my heart overflowed with joy and gratitude. I rushed outside

lives of perhaps countless others? I had no words to say as my spirit sat softly by me, wordlessly holding my hand.

"*Reflecting the experiences of your life, I am Raag Jhinjhoti*", said the vision in a low and soft voice.

"*In me you will find those moments that you hoped would never go away and those moments that you wished you would never experience.*

For every moment in life there is a musical note. Few hear the sound; few know they are part of a great orchestra, so busy are they living through that moment in preparation for the next. Something magical will happen next, this is only the prelude, they think. And they are right. But in their haste they fail to hear the lovely harmonics of the moments in which they live.

When your young mother gave birth to you, I was in attendance, my Shadaj wrapping you in a warm invisible blanket of love. Perhaps you opened your eyes then and saw me! So I decided to remain and do more.

Ah, your happy laughs! Your delight in the playing of simple games with your brother and sister! It continued till other pressures of life nudged them aside. Shuddha Rishabh, Shuddha Madhyam and Shuddha Gandhar reflected my understanding.

Your dazed incomprehension when you experienced your first final parting - was it the old grandmother who you thought would never leave you? That rock of love?....... Who could answer your questions? Who could meet your demand that she should come back immediately? I was there and comforted you, though you did not know. Do you remember that snatch of emotion in Komal Nishad, Shuddha Dhaivat, Pancham and Shuddha Madhyam? And when you finally reconciled to the unbearable loss, I added Shuddha Gandhar, Shuddha Rishabh and Shadaj and the phrase was complete.

In me is your devotion to God, intense one day, invisible the next. Shuddha Gandhar is plaintive one moment and placid the next. I moved up the octaves as you went through misery and had the intelligence to pray to the power that made you. See Pancham, Shuddha Dhaivat, Shadaj,

Shuddha Rishabh and Shuddha Gandhar.

And when you resolved to learn music and dance, I knew no limits to my joy. I, your Guardian angel, danced like a calf enjoying its first spring. Here one moment and then there the next! You actually whistled one day as you walked to your teacher's house and I floated into the air on your breath. What was that tune? Shuddha Gandhar, Shuddha Madhyam, Shuddha Rishabh, Shuddha Gandhar, Shadaj, Shuddha Rishabh, Shuddha Nishad and Shadaj. Like water gushing on steps and falling, falling......

Your marriage and your children.... You dared compare yourself to Krishna and your wife to Radha. And why would you not? In Banaras and Mathura, hear the wonderful tunes that form around me. Those were the days you felt you were living life to its fullest, surrounded by people who needed you and cared for you.

At times of despair, at times of hopeless agony, you appealed to men or God using me. Pancham, Shuddha Dhaivat, Shadaj, Shuddha Rishabh and Shuddha Gandhar. See how the sequence wafts upwards, taking your appeal for justice to the court of Indra. With Shadaj, Shuddha Rishabh, Komal Nishad, Shuddha Dhaivat and Pancham, you marked resignation and acceptance. Your belief in destiny was strengthened and you lost the will to fight beyond a point. Pancham, Shuddha Dhaivat, Shuddha Madhyam and Shuddha Gandhar, slow and lingering, capture your final transition to maturity and the recognition of the transience of life.

Throughout, you returned to Shuddha Gandhar, like a tenuous rope tied between the points of birth and death. And with Komal Nishad, bridged with Shadaj, you built the foundation of a life of love and sacrifice, tolerance and yielding. Yes, I was there.

As you watched the flames consume the remains of your wife, I was with you, mixed with the tears that fell to earth. I am slow, with pathos, understanding you perhaps better than you understand yourself.

I am Raag Jhinjhoti, the Raag of Memories. You cannot forget me and I cannot forget you"

So saying, the apparition that was I, dissolved. My grief threatened to tear me apart as wave after wave of both sad and happy memories completely submerged me.

I warned you, said my tearful spirit, I warned you but you did not listen.

In the gloaming, I could hear myself sing, though no sound came from my lips.

P D S R M G... S R n D
R M P D S R n D P
D P M G R
S R n D ....M P D M G
S R n D S

or months afterwards, my spirit and I chose not to touch each other. Jhinjhoti had been sublimely moving; the Raag had captured everything that I had experienced in life and played it all back to me. I did not have the strength to recover from its magic. I felt as though the spiritual strengths that I thought I had acquired from the combination of meditation and music had been sapped. I felt weak, unable to bear even the slightest sound of anything resembling music.

Philosophical thought seemed arcane and devoid of any sense. Pain rent my heart as all the memories deep within, those which I had thought were faded with time, came gushing back as though the events had happened only yesterday. It seemed as if I was two years old, then sixteen, then thirty-one, then fifty-six, then seventy, and then eighty-two. I had been transported simultaneously into thousands of different points in my life's journey. My memories were real again and the consequences were devastating.

But slowly I regained my composure. I no longer blamed the Raag; after all, I had invoked it against the better judgement of my own spirit. I caressed it again, seeking forgiveness. And my spirit, being my own, forgave me.

We retraced our journey through the musical wonderland of India. Sorathdesa and Ramkali - the Raags of piety and tranquillity. Bageshree and Patdip - Raags redolent with romance and love. The Sarangs - full of life and vigour. Puriyadhanashri - serious and mystical. Chandrakauns and Kamod - lyrical and sweet. Bhatiyar and Megh - the sounds of water. What a lovely tapestry! Who was this heavenly weaver who could toy with these sounds and create designs not meant for mortals?

I brought out my Tanpura, gently wiping it clean of the dust that had accumulated due to neglect. I had no aim in mind. I wished to continue demonstrating my respect for music, asking nothing in return. I did not feel I had been blessed, at least in this lifetime, to handle the exquisite and intricate designs of the hundreds of Raags that I knew were hidden within the Tanpura and also in the air, invisible.

My spirit too felt that the journey ought to end with dignity. Too much had been asked. So much had been given. We did not deserve such blessings and such revelations. We were still on this tiny earth, drifting through space, of absolutely no consequence to the Almighty. Enough, it said, enough! The Tanpura alone will do. Nothing more. We are too weak and useless to delve any deeper into the mysteries of the Raags.

I wiped the Tanpura clean. I knew instinctively that it was still in perfect tune. But I did not have the courage to touch the strings. Who knew what cataclysm might be unleashed if the strings resonated together?

I placed it with utmost respect at the far end of the room. There it was, a gift of the divine, crafted, strangely enough, by men. I wondered if they had any inkling of what they had wrought.

My spirit and I sat together and stared for hours together at the Tanpura. We felt weak and insipid. My limbs ached, I knew not why. Every movement was an effort. Perhaps age was finally catching up. I did not resist. My journey was perhaps at an end and music had lit the path throughout. I had been a lonely traveller, unable to share my love for music with anyone. The joys were private even if universal. I had been condemned to suffer and listen to the wordless messages in the Raags that I had met. I was not an artiste. I was not a critic. I was nothing. And yet I suffered.

But at length, my spirit and I, after looking at each other wordlessly for some time, stretched forward and once again - very tentatively - slowly plucked the strings of the Tanpura.

The room lit up with sound. Moving from wall to wall, Shadaj and Pancham covered every corner of the room with their divine comfort. They seemed to stop in front of me and placed their hands gently on my head. They understood my torment. They understood my plight.

I closed my eyes, trembling. What had I done? Once again, the electrifying power of the Raags threatened to enmesh me. And if that happened, I knew that I would be completely destroyed. My body was too weak, my spirit almost lifeless.

Those magical notes reverberated through the room for a long time. My panic vanished gradually and once again I found balance and poise. I closed my eyes and reclaimed, little by little, my ability to meditate without being disturbed by stray thoughts. The same notes that had driven me to distraction had also lovingly given peace back to me.

The image of Shiva in meditation came to me. Raag Bhairav and its accompanying deep connotations were swirling about Shiva in my mind's eye. Sound and rhythm lay at his feet, waiting to do as he bid. Time went by, without being noticed or even wanted. I lost myself in contemplation of this wondrous Lord and all that he stood for.

And lo! A white light came from his body and fell on my mind. Feminine and soft, it caressed my heart with love.

I opened my eyes. The Tanpura itself was transforming. Ripples of light enveloped it and the Tanpura disappeared. In its place was Bhairavi herself.

She sat bedecked in red and green. From her lotus eyes flowed compassion and insight. In her lap were all the Raags of which she was the mother. Behind her was the palace of her father, Himavan, who presided over the

Himalayas.

"You who seek", she said, *"You are blessed. After searching for some meaning to this existence to which you have been condemned for past sins, you have understood that music is the answer.*

See the seven notes, rings on my fingers. See the flowers that lie at my feet, each a different Raag, each with a different fragrance. If you wish to smell each flower, you will not finish in this lifetime or the next.

From the unyielding but affectionate Bhairav have I come. My husband has given me the gift of creating Raags and playing with the notes. Seek no other Raag after me. I contain all of them and more. After me there is nothing, absolutely nothing.

First I have softened the Shuddha Gandhar and Shuddha Nishad. In my courtyard, I want all the notes to be in attendance should I require them. Perhaps I wish to worship Shiva differently today and I would use Teevra Madhyam. Who can stop me?

When you smell the jasmine that also says Komal Nishad, Shadaj, Komal Gandhar, Shadaj and Komal Rishabh and Shadaj, you will know that I am present. I tease my divine husband by using his Komal Rishabh and raising it by half a note to Shuddha Rishabh. He does not mind and smiles benignly because I always give it back to him, as pure as it was when I took it away. I remember him in everything I do with Shadaj, Komal Rishabh and Shadaj.

Shadaj, Komal Rishabh and Shuddha Madhyam - I remind you of all the Raags that I can give you, of all the Raags you have met. And I touch Teevra Madhyam gliding down to Komal Gandhar and Komal Rishabh and back to Komal Gandhar, because I know that no one will ever be able to take everything I am willing to give. But take them if you wish, my son, take them.

Pancham is the note of happiness and I use it when I tell the stories of creation to my children, the Raags. And then with Komal Dhaivat and Shuddha Madhyam, I put them to sleep so that I can whisper other secrets into their ears.

Komal Gandhar, Shuddha Rishabh, Komal Gandhar and Shadaj, Komal

Rishabh and Shadaj - these are the two offerings of Bilva leaves I place at the feet of Shiva, the All Powerful.

Komal Nishad, ever meek but full of wisdom, I bring to those who worship me. Use it gently and without hurry because it will help you reach Shadaj and Komal Rishabh without whom I cannot exist, made as I am of and by Shiva.

In my hair, find the thousands of combinations of my notes sprinkled as flowers. Their fragrance will drive you mad. You cannot escape from my loving embrace.

Komal Dhaivat, Pancham and Shuddha Madhyam are my feet, aiding me as I create hymns in praise of Shiva even when he asks for no such offering.

Do not go here and there searching for elusive treasures. I contain them all - the known, the unexpected. My jewels are for you, but you must ask, and forever remain humble. But once I give, your soul is mine too.

For ever."

As Mother Bhairavi vanished and the Tanpura returned, I found that I was at complete peace. I had seen the emotions in her. I knew there was no hope of ever learning everything she was willing to teach. But I was drenched in a strange feeling of absolute peace and satisfaction.

The room still had the faint echoes of her fragrance.

> n S g M P d P ..... R g M g r S
>
> d - M r S
>
> r g r n d P......
>
> S R g r S

My spirit and I sat, holding hands. The time had come. Our explorations into the Universe of Raags had come to an end. We were humbler, more respectful, yes. But I felt I knew something of what the Raags had to offer. Perhaps in my next lifetime, I would learn even more; my heart surged with happiness at that thought.

I bade a fond and happy Goodbye to my own spirit, thanking it for showing me so much. It re-entered me quietly and I was whole again.

And I prostrated in front of the holy Tanpura.

Raag Basant

Aaroh	S G m d N r⌃ S⌃
Avroh	S⌃ N d P - m G- m G r S

Raag Brindavani Sarang

Aaroh	S R M P N S⌃
Avroh	S⌃ n P M R S, ̣N S

Raag Bageshree

Aaroh	S g M D n S⌃
Avroh	S⌃ n D M P D g R ̣n S

Raag Bhairav

Aaroh	S r G M P d N S⌃
Avroh	S⌃ N d P M G r S

Raag Bhairavi

Aaroh	S r g M P d n S⌃
Avroh	S⌃ n d P M g r S

Raag Bhatiyar

| Aaroh | S M P D N D S⁺ |
| Avroh | r⁺ S⁺ N D P M, P G r S |

Raag Chandrakauns

| Aaroh | S g M d N S⁺ |
| Avroh | S⁺ N d M g M g S N d S |

Raag Charukesi

| Aaroh | S R G M P d n S⁺ |
| Avroh | S⁺ n d P M G R S |

Raag Gaur Sarang

| Aaroh | N S R S - G R M - G P - m P D N S⁺ |
| Avroh | S⁺ N D P - m P D N P - D P - M G R S |

Raag Jogiya

| Aaroh | S r M P d S⁺ |
| Avroh | S⁺ N d P M M r S d r r S |

Raag Jaijaiwanti

Aaroh	S RgRS͜ NSRmPNS⌃
Avroh	S⌃nDP MG RgR͜nS͜D͜nRS

Raag Jhinjhoti

Aaroh	SRMPDS⌃
Avroh	S⌃nDPMGRS,R͜n͜DS

Raag Kamod

Aaroh	SRP GmSRS-MPDNS⌃
Avroh	S⌃NDP- mPDP- GMP-GMSRS

Raag Malkauns

Aaroh	SgMdnS⌃
Avroh	S⌃ndMgS

Raag Mand

Aaroh	SRGMPDNPDS⌃
Avroh	S⌃NDPMGRGS

Raag Megh

Aaroh	S n nS, RMPn PnnS⁺
Avroh	S⁺nPMPnPMR-RPmR- n nS

Raag Patdip

Aaroh	NSgMPNS⁺
Avroh	S⁺NDPMgRS NS

Raag Puriyadhanashri

Aaroh	NrGmPd NS⁺
Avroh	S⁺NdPmGmrGr S

Raag Ramkali

Aaroh	S rGMPdNS⁺
Avroh	S⁺NdPmPdn dPGM rS

Raag Shuddha Sarang

Aaroh	NSRMPNS⁺
Avroh	S⁺NDPmPMSRS

Raag Sorathdesa

Aaroh	SRMPNS⁺
Avroh	S⁺R⁺nDPDMGR NS